7.

road, your journey, y
life.

Cliff

Confessions on the Road to Real

Life in the Slow Lane

Cliff Bond

WestBow Press
A DIVISION OF THOMAS NELSON
& ZONDERVAN

Copyright © 2014 Cliff Bond.

All rights reserved. No part of this book may be used or reproduced by any means, graphic, electronic, or mechanical, including photocopying, recording, taping or by any information storage retrieval system without the written permission of the publisher except in the case of brief quotations embodied in critical articles and reviews.

WestBow Press books may be ordered through booksellers or by contacting:

WestBow Press
A Division of Thomas Nelson
1663 Liberty Drive
Bloomington, IN 47403
www.westbowpress.com
1 (866) 928-1240

Scripture taken from the King James Version of the Bible.

Scriptures taken from the Holy Bible, New International Version®, NIV®. Copyright © 1973, 1978, 1984, 2011 by Biblica, Inc.™ Used by permission of Zondervan. All rights reserved worldwide. www.zondervan.com The "NIV" and "New International Version" are trademarks registered in the United States Patent and Trademark Office by Biblica, Inc.™ All rights reserved.

Because of the dynamic nature of the Internet, any web addresses or links contained in this book may have changed since publication and may no longer be valid. The views expressed in this work are solely those of the author and do not necessarily reflect the views of the publisher, and the publisher hereby disclaims any responsibility for them.

Any people depicted in stock imagery provided by Thinkstock are models, and such images are being used for illustrative purposes only.
Certain stock imagery © Thinkstock.

ISBN: 978-1-4908-2009-5 (sc)
ISBN: 978-1-4908-2010-1 (hc)
ISBN: 978-1-4908-2008-8 (e)

Library of Congress Control Number: 2013922862

Printed in the United States of America.

WestBow Press rev. date: 01/28/2014

Contents

Introduction vii
"Son, You Look Like a Minister!" 1
"Honey, Something's Wrong!" 4
"You Would Think It Was God Who Died" 11
"I'm Sorry Your Son Died" 16
"You Can Do That?" 20
Discerning of Spirits 26
"What Can I Do For You?" 31
Breaking Rules 36
Explosions 42
"I Have Nothing to Say" 47
Spirituality 52
"Thank You Jesus!" 58
"I Can't Trust You Anymore" 63
"So, What Is The Exact Nature of My Wrongs?" 67
"Oops—Wrong Room!" 73
"Who Are YOU?!" 78
"Our Parents Are Not Perfect" 83
Faith, Family, Friends 89
"Whatever It Is You Do…" 94
"Should" Is the Word of Death 98
"Go and Sin Some More" 104
"Rhonda's" Story 110

"This Is Not Good" 119
"Oh There You Are—I Knew You'd Find Me!" 125
Three Little Words 130
"I Will Never Again Settle For Less" 135
"I Love You to Pieces, Even If You Are a Baptist" 140
Realistic Hope 145
Learning From a Lady 150
"I Promise You…" 166
"You Are Forgiven" 171
Postscript 179
Suggested reading, ... 181

Introduction

My name is Bond, Cliff Bond. I have been blessed by having a woman love me for over fifty years, and we've been married since September 5, 1964. This woman is one of the most realistic people I've ever met which is partly due to her training as a registered nurse and partly just the way she is. When I flounder around trying to find words, she says, "Why don't you just say it?" and lo and behold, she is right.

Being real is not a simple task. We are taught subterfuge and dishonesty from an early age. We seldom say what we mean or mean what we say. We ask "How are you?" and are answered dishonestly, most of the time, with "Fine." One of my professors said to his students that when we are preaching to a congregation, remember that at least forty percent are deeply sad or depressed at that moment. And yet, they will usually look very well indeed. We're not transparently real with others, and we're not consistently honest with ourselves.

Stories of my ministry are all entirely true, although names are disguised to maintain confidentiality. They are not all easily told but that is part of being real. The individual chapters are intended to be free-standing narratives so there will be repeated information common to more than one chapter. The stories are not always in chronological order, which is intentional because insight doesn't come in a linear format but appears in surprises and intrusions into our orderly lives. The meditations interspersed in the text are by my wonderful wife, Carol, whose words bring me back, time and time again, to the real essence of existence and faith. Her words are tough and not flowery. They, like her, are real, and it is to her and her real nature that this book is dedicated.

It is my hope that you, as a reader of my stories, will take them for what they are—unfinished glimpses into a process, not a completed work. These are confessions of a struggle toward a goal that won't be reached in this brief existence we call life. If you find encouragement that helps on your journey, then I am satisfied. If any of the writing sounds too much like "school" or "teaching," I do most sincerely apologize. The only time I like "how to" books is when I'm building an engine or doing some other technical task. "How to" work with people is a bit more complex than that. No one-size-fits-all solution exists. I find that working with a person in crisis takes much more attention than any other interaction I have ever had. It is those times when we are called upon to be authentically real, open, honest, and willing that bring out the best, or the worst, of what and who we really are.

I owe my wife so much on my journey. She is one of the most honest people I've ever met and one of the most practical. Her writings, meditations, and poems strike to the heart of reality and are not always soothing so much as they are challenging or even confrontive. The few examples of her work included in this book will bless you—if you allow it. But they, like the theme here, are attempts to be real, and reality is not always pleasant to examine.

I grew up during the '50s and '60s when cars were involved in a horsepower race that was intoxicating. My buddies and I looked under the hood of every car we could and then looked inside to see how high the speedometer numbers went. "How fast will it go?"

was the question we asked. When I was old enough to buy my own car, I had several that were fast and loud. I witnessed the births of the Corvette, the Hemi, the T-bird, the Mustang, the Camaro, the 'Cuda, the AMX, and many other fast and loud machines. I bragged about how quickly I could get from Cedar Rapids, Iowa, to Kansas City, Kansas, where my fiancé went to nursing school. That was back before the interstate highways were completed, so much of my driving was through little towns and on two-lane highways, which meant lots of "passing." Eventually I even built engines for my own car that I drag raced at Heartland Park Topeka in the quarter mile from 1999–2004. But, even though I love fast cars, I found speed wasn't good in all things. Life couldn't be pushed too hard and, when it came to becoming a real person, fast wasn't always the best way to go. I began to learn, primarily from others, that life sets its own pace. It's this "slow lane" discovery I've chronicled here.

Years ago I became friends with the children's book, "The Velveteen Rabbit" by Margery Williams. What does it mean to be real? We are real, the old skin horse says, when we are loved. That is scarier than it sounds because to be loved, he says, is to have our fur rubbed off in spots and maybe to lose an eye or have hairs pulled from our tail. It costs to be real. But it is worth it. At least I haven't lost an eye yet.

That's a good explanation for a children's book, but what about real life? What does it mean to become real? The theme of this book is that it takes the same thing. Being real happens only when we allow ourselves to be loved. Notice, I said, when we ALLOW ourselves to be loved. There is a cost. And it takes a lot of time. So, the journey to real is told in the format of confessions, of discoveries, of struggles, of failures, and of successes. All are essential ingredients to becoming real. Neal Diamond said, "Being lost is worth the being found," poetic talk for how hard the journey is to become real.

We were allowed to have four wonderful children, each of whom has influenced our lives and enriched us in different ways. To these children, Craig, Clay, Camille and Cory, I say you are a blessing beyond measure and I thank you for supporting your minister dad as he found his path and followed it. You never doubted me, even when I doubted myself.

Along the way I've been privileged to share in the lives of many other pilgrims on this same road. There are more than one might think, and they come from all walks of life, each gender, every ethnic group, all religions, every relational persuasion, every age, and every everything. In common, we have a desire to be more and to remain always dissatisfied with who and what we are at any given moment. We know we're not entirely real and that's okay. To these fellow travelers, I owe a great debt of gratitude because you have bumped into my life and left me feeling uneasy. Thank you. I will not begin to name names because the list is long. You will hear echoes of your lives in what I write so look for your wisdom because if you shared it with me, I have used it in my own journey. Thank you, again.

And then there is the God of my understanding. I know my theology is inadequate but that also is okay. My concept of God changes continually but it goes deeper, not shallower. I believe in a God who is also real, not just in existence but primarily in relationship. I couldn't function without that understanding of God. Like Popeye said in the cartoon, "I yam what I yam!" And God is who God is. Beyond that we are just scratching the surface.

In the pages of this book, you'll find stories of how I came to my understanding of God. The stories aren't pretty, all the time, but they are real. Christianity is not pretty all the time either. It deals not only with promise but with suffering, death, sacrifice, and hardship. We make it pretty in our churches and cathedrals, which is acceptable only if we remember the sacraments we celebrate are indeed about a broken body and shed blood. No, it is not pretty at all, but it is beautiful as only reality can be. So, God of my understanding, this book is really about you and how you entered into my experience and brought about wonders and miracles that leave me breathless. Lord, you amaze me.

Cliff Bond, chaplain
Topeka, KS
2013
blessingsonyourjourney.com

A special word about my friend and editor, Morgan Chilson. She cleaned up my manuscript without altering my writing style. www.exactlywrite.net turned what was at first a very intimidating task for me, into an extremely rewarding experience. Thank you, Morgan.

"Son, You Look Like a Minister!"

By the time I was seven years old, I was preaching to my four-year-old sister from a stump in the middle of a lilac bush. I don't remember any of the topics, but my sister says she enjoyed my "sermons." As a child, I stood behind the pulpit in our church and wondered what it would be like to stand there and be tall enough to look over it at a congregation who eagerly anticipated what I had to say. By age twelve, I was baptized but decided I would wait until I was old—at least thirty—before giving my life to God. I wanted to have some fun and games first.

By the age of twenty, I completed two years of college toward a Bachelor of Science in medical technology. I still had occasional thoughts of being a missionary someday, but that was put on hold by my need to achieve gainful employment to support myself and my wife-to-be in our plans for marriage the following year. In that summer of 1963, I joined with college classmates to work a summer job selling books and Bibles door-to-door in Mineral Wells, Texas. I'd been told this would be an easy way to make lots of money. I did well for the first couple of months and then became discouraged and even "burned out" in the heat and the tedium of going door-to-door as a salesman. I'd been run off of various properties, had dogs set on me, was cheated by some of my customers and treated poorly by some of the nice church people who lived in that area. It was a slice of reality that made me wish I was home in Kansas. Then the engine in my car gave up the ghost in the Texas heat and what little money I earned as a salesman went into replacing that engine so I could return home.

In that very downtrodden state of mind, I prayed one morning before setting out to knock on doors that if God wanted me to be a pastor, I needed to hear it clearly and promptly. I was now in one of the less prosperous areas of that part of Texas, and the first home I came to was more of a shack than a house. Nevertheless, I dutifully knocked. An old man came to the door, looked at me and said, "Son, you look like a minister!" It took a few seconds for me to respond but I looked at him and managed to say, "Why did you say that?" He looked right through me and said, "I don't know—the Lord just told me to say it." He invited me in and we talked. I don't remember if he bought anything or not. I was far too shocked in getting what I felt was a direct answer to my prayer.

A few weeks later, I returned to Kansas before driving to Iowa where I had arranged to work with my uncle in his drywall company, hanging and finishing sheetrock in new house construction. My plans to complete training as a medical technologist were now put on hold because of my financial situation. I spent 1963, and part of 1964, working for my uncle when several other events happened that impacted my life as well. I can still remember the moment I heard on the car radio that President Kennedy was shot and killed. That event shocked me and made me re-evaluate my priorities. In addition to that, my uncle was a pastor of a small church and had been a major influence on my life before this. I began to think once again about becoming a minister. I contacted several Bible Colleges, was licensed to preach by my home church in Kansas, and then in 1964 I was called up for the draft at Fort Des Moines. Of course, I passed my physical but since I was licensed to preach and was now enrolled in Bible College for the fall of 1964, I received a 4-D classification, meaning I wouldn't be called up right away.

So, now my life had come full circle back to my beginnings of ministry from lilac bush to Bible College. I was going to train to be a minister. My fiancé graduated from nursing school in September, we were married, and our plans included becoming medical missionaries. I was beginning to look more and more like a minister. Maybe that old man in Mineral Wells was right. Yes, I still remember his name and although he has long ago gone to be with his Lord, I am very glad he was listening to God's voice and then became God's voice in reminding me what I had forgotten. My adventure was just beginning but I was ready, or at least I felt as if I was. In any case, the journey began for me. The "slow lane" was picking up speed.

"Honey, Something's Wrong!"

My wife and I started dating in the winter of 1959 and were going steady within a year, at which time I gave her a friendship ring. (Like the Elvis song said, "Won't you wear my ring around your neck to tell the world you're mine by heck.") She was one year ahead of me in school, graduating from high school in 1960 while I graduated in 1961. We were very much in love and made plans to get married after she completed nursing school in 1964. I planned to train as a pastor so we could be a missionary couple at our denomination's mission station in Malawi, Africa. We married in September 1964, and she worked full time as a nurse while I worked part time as a gas station attendant (yes; that was back when gas stations were really service stations) and went to school at Calvary Bible College in Kansas City. Our plans changed a bit when Carol became pregnant. We had our first child, Craig Alan, and suddenly became a family. I went to work full time, first as a mechanic at the service station and then as pastor of our Seventh Day Baptist Church in Kansas City, which also allowed me to continue my schooling at Calvary Bible College.

We wanted our children to be close together in age, so we planned our next pregnancy to continue our family as soon as possible. This second pregnancy was problematic with many difficulties. On the night of October 31, 1966, Carol awakened me exactly at midnight (I remember looking at the clock) and said, "Honey, something is wrong!" Indeed there was. She was bleeding a great deal and so we rushed to the hospital. After a long and very painful labor, during which Carol almost died and the baby did die of multiple birth defects, we had our second son, Clay Dwight. We had his funeral a few days later after we gave his little body to KU Medical Center so doctors in training could learn how to treat birth defects and save lives of other children in the future. We felt it was the right decision to make. We learned later they kept him until 1991 when his remains were respectfully cremated and buried at Lawrence, Kansas. Carol and I have both worked in health care for most of our lives, and we wonder how many doctors benefited from our precious gift to their training experience.

A year later we had a daughter, Camille Cathleen, to add to our growing family and yes, the children were close in age and in relationship. We left the Kansas City church and took on the pastorate of two small churches in Rhode Island, requiring a major move on our part. Carol had an uncle, who was also a pastor, not far away and their family helped us during our time in New England. We were still thinking of going to Africa as missionaries and were making arrangements with the denominational leaders to do so. However, Carol was pregnant again because we wanted more children. This time, the Rh factor came into play since Carol was negative and I was positive. The child was in crisis during the entire pregnancy, which required monitoring by amniocentesis once a week to determine how severely he was affected. Each painful test required a trip to specialists at Yale/New Haven Hospital during the winter months, usually on snowy roads. The doctor recommended inducing labor in March 1969 and our son, Cory Michael, was born. He looked perfectly normal even though his blood was being destroyed by the Rh reaction. After three complete blood exchanges and several weeks in intensive care, he came home to his parents and two older siblings. We were so glad to have him. We also knew we would be wise to have no more pregnancies because of the Rh reality. To this day, we are gratefully indebted to three complete strangers who came from many miles away to give of their lifeblood, the required rare type, to save the life of our son. Our family was now complete.

It was a very difficult situation for us all because the medical needs during this last pregnancy and birth blocked our plans to go to Malawi. Another couple went to the mission station, ending our earlier dreams. We were emotionally overloaded from the past few years of birth, sickness, and death, so we left the pastorate, returning to Kansas where I contacted my prior employers. They now had a car dealership in Olathe, Kansas, instead of a filling station, and I worked there as a mechanic and car detailer until there was an opening for parts manager that I took. Things were improving in some ways but my inner world was one of suppressed anger and hurt, feelings that had not been resolved by being busy as a pastor or by moving halfway across the country to escape painful memories. I wasn't aware, consciously, of that inner world but others around me were. I wasn't always patient with my young children or with my lovely wife who had lost so much. I am not particularly proud of that time, but I did try to do the best I could. I just was unable to process or resolve the powerful feelings of grief and loss that were consuming me.

One day at work I felt sick to my stomach and went outside the shop building where I promptly began vomiting blood—lots of blood. I staggered back inside looking absolutely ghastly so my boss sent me home to my nurse wife who took one look at me and phoned our doctor—the doctor who had delivered Craig, Clay, and Camille. He was a person who knew us best and whom we trusted completely. He ordered an ambulance, which rushed me to Kansas City in a March snowstorm in 1971. I was admitted to Intensive Care where the medical team stabilized me allowing me to return home a week later on some new medications including valium to quiet my anger. The valium worked. It actually worked too well and during the coming months I became very unconcerned about the needs of work, home or relationships. Carol called it "numzit" because I was emotionally numb. I did not know it, but I had become addicted to the valium even though at that time it was considered safe and non-addictive. My wife eventually helped me taper the dose in early 1972. After several weeks of that "detox" I was off that medication although still on some others which helped with stomach acid. My eating habits changed but I was able to lead a normal life with minimal problems.

After several years of success at the dealership I was promoted to service manager, and given a new car to drive as well as a percentage of the shop profit as a bonus. We were financially secure and doing well in other ways also. But there was still "something wrong." We had wanted to be a missionary couple. We had planned on my being a pastor. We were active in our home church in Nortonville, Kansas, and I also worked part time as a pastor in Kansas City, but our dream of service wasn't quite complete. We couldn't go to the mission field, but we as a family talked it over, and the outcome was a decision for me to go back to school. We had financial, emotional, and spiritual support from various family members and our home church, which was so very important and encouraging to us. After completing my undergraduate degree at Baker University in 1978 at Baldwin City, Kansas, we made the decision to move to Atlanta, Georgia, where Carol worked as a nurse so I could complete a three-year master's program to train as a clinical chaplain.

After that, we returned to Kansas in 1981 where I completed a year internship before being hired as a counselor/chaplain at Bethany

Medical Center. That position was dissolved in 1983 so I was once again working for a car dealership, this time in Lawrence, Kansas. "Honey, something's wrong" happened again. Had we totally misunderstood God's will?

By this time, our children were in high school and our financial situation was bleak. Carol and I both lost jobs, and we began questioning decisions made that didn't seem to be working out. Truly, it seemed that again, "something was wrong." Eventually, I was hired as a chaplain at Saint Francis Hospital in Topeka, Kansas, in 1984. Carol worked as a nurse for the State of Kansas and later for an eye surgeon, before finishing out her career at the Shawnee County Health Department in 2002. I retired from Saint Francis in 2006 but continued working for hospice agencies full or part time for another three years. At the time of this writing, I work two days a week as counselor/chaplain at a local addiction recovery treatment center and one day a week as chaplain at a cancer treatment center. I guess I am "semi" retired.

The words, "Honey, something's wrong," uttered powerfully those many years ago, became a family theme through the years. Many things in life are significantly wrong, and many people are affected by those wrongs. The death of our son eventually resulted in the motivation to learn how to first heal our own hurt and then to find ways of helping others with their hurt when things go wrong. Both Carol and I worked in health care, not as we had planned back in 1960, but we became "missionaries" anyway, here at home. There will always be "something wrong" in our lives and in the lives of those around us. There will always be losses, diseases, deaths, hardships, addictions, and much more. We as a family experienced some of the wrongs and we survived. Our family is strong and we were made stronger in some ways because of our experiences. But the events themselves weren't good. God helped us through the losses, but the losses weren't good things.

We were told, when Clay died, that this was part of God's plan and we shouldn't grieve. There is some truth to that, but there is also much error. We tried to bury our grief, but it just came out sideways. The death of a child is wrong. To say it is part of God's plan is partly true but also totally mistaken. Scripture says many things and taking one verse out of context can "prove" almost anything. The fact is that Jesus spent his energy healing what was wrong. If wrongs are "God's will," then he was fighting against God when he healed people.

The wrongs are still wrong, but God can and does create something good out of even the worst wrong. That is the lesson we learned, painfully and slowly, after Clay's death. Don't ever say to me that I am lucky or blessed to have had a son die. Don't go there. His death was not a blessing and it was not the will of God that killed Clay at midnight on Halloween in 1966. I believe in evil just as surely as I believe in good.

Many things in life are wrong. Thankfully, God helped us find a way to fight against the wrongs and to make a difference. Eldridge Cleaver said we have a choice in life. We can be either part of the problem or part of the solution. Only the solutions are a good thing. The problems are still wrong. Don't ever confuse the two. God doesn't.

I Need to Talk--

      Hello God, it's me again...
      I'd like to talk a little while
I need someone who'll listen
To my troubles and my woes ...

   And pick me up when I wander, stumble or fall.

      You see, I can't quite make it
Through the day just on my own...
      For I feel so lost and oh so tired
      I'd really like to just quit trying...

   And stop and let someone else worry about stuff.

      I'd like to believe in you more and fully trust...
      But I'm not sure of me or You or anything...
      The past, the present and future fret me...
         Anger, reality, fear and dreams agitate and I'm confused...

   And I wonder is there really hope out there?

    This faith thing...belief, trust, honor, worship
      Doing right, caring for self and others
      Is difficult at best for logic is often baffled
         My mind is chaotic as I struggle with what I've experienced

      And seek what you would have me be and what your Word really teaches.

   Help me not to worry over things I can't change in any way.
      You have so many to listen to I wonder...
      Can you hear my quavering voice amidst the din of us all?
         My faith is often weak and I ask...are you there?

   And yet I talk to you in prayer and it keeps me sane and going.

      In closing I'd like to ask you please to keep
   My family, loved ones and me safe in your care.
Come and fill our lives with faith and love for you and fellow travelers.
         Give us confidence to face each of our life's journeys

   And to be strong whatever comes our way in life.

      Blessings to you God
      Thanks for being there!

Carol A. Bond

Cliff Bond

"You Would Think It Was God Who Died"

There are many ways to handle the grief that comes with the loss of a loved one. None of us know how until we do it, and even then, we usually don't do it smoothly. My wife and I are certainly no exception, although we were expected to grieve well because I was a pastor and she was the pastor's wife. Right or wrong, fair or unfair, reasonable or not, we do have higher expectations of some people than we do of others. When it comes to faith in God, we expect the leaders of the Church to do better than those outside that position.

When our son died we were devastated. We had donated his body to KU Medical Center so there was no body for a conventional funeral. Yet Carol and I wanted a memorial service anyway to commemorate his short life, and one was planned. Some family members asked us why we were putting ourselves through that. A pastor friend summed it up very well when he said to us, "The way you two are acting, you would think it was God who died!" That was very direct and it caused us significant guilt and shame making us wonder if we were indeed doing too much grieving. We wondered if we needed to just get over it and continue with our family planning and forget all about this unfortunate incident. In effect, we thought maybe the level of grief we experienced showed a lack of faith. Other chapters in this book go into more detail about that process, but here I want to explore what was said and how it connects to how we in our society often deal with death and dying—because it does connect.

Dr. Alan Wolfelt presents seminars on grief and loss for professionals in healthcare. I have attended several and find his information very helpful. I shared what the minister said about God dying with him during one of his sessions, and he agreed that it was symbolic of how we in the religious community often handle grief. We want to grieve but we also want to be strong in the faith, trust God, and believe everything happens for a reason and everything is part of God's plan.

I no longer believe grief and faith are necessarily mutually exclusive. Is it appropriate to tell a patient dying of cancer that this is God's will and we should not, therefore, pray for healing? Do we tell the family member of a child who is killed in a car accident that this is part of God's plan? Was the slaughter of millions in WWII God's will? Are earthquakes and tidal waves part of God's plan? We could answer yes or no and still be at least partially correct. And perhaps we would also be completely wrong. It is just not that simple. God has often intervened to bring relief from suffering and death. As an example, Jesus didn't accept blindness as God's will. He quite bluntly told the religious leaders, who said it was, that they were completely mistaken. (John 9:3)

My pastor friend did us, and himself, no favors when he said what he did. I don't blame him or hold him in contempt for what he said. I agree there needs to be a balance, but I do believe he had the balance way too far toward acceptance and not close enough to intervention. The Serenity Prayer suggests that we "accept the things we cannot change, change the things we can, and have the wisdom to know the difference." That is just a pretty good balance. For myself, I reword it slightly to fit my personality and say I will "accept the things I cannot change, change the things I cannot accept, and have the wisdom to know the difference." My rewording is a bit more aggressive, but then, I believe ministry needs to be assertive, not passive.

Did Carol and I do the right thing in having a memorial service for our stillborn son or was it okay to avoid that because his body wasn't there and so "out of sight, out of mind"? Clay was our child, our son, who was physically connected to my wife's body for nine months. His heart beat close to hers. Half of his genetics came from me. He was, quite literally, flesh of our flesh and bone of our bone. He was our son and he died. It was right, proper, correct, and spiritual for us to have a memorial service. And yet, we second guessed ourselves and felt guilty for many years because of what others said about our grieving so much, when we were supposed to be people of faith and leaders of the people of faith as pastor and wife.

In 2004, Carol and I were in Washington, D.C., for an addiction seminar. While there we saw the Lincoln Memorial, the WWII memorial, the one for Korea, and the Black Wall for Vietnam Vets. We walked through Arlington National Cemetery and witnessed the changing of the guard at the Tomb of the Unknown Soldier. Why did we put ourselves through that? Were we acting as though God had died because we were at a place that honors the dead? Were we giving up hope because of the high emotion we felt at those places of honor? Just what would it mean to behave as though God had died?

But wait, as some TV ads say, "There's more!" Those words uttered at the time of our son's death were said by a very fundamental Christian minister who believed Jesus is the Son of God and was God in the Flesh who died to save humanity from their sins. Now wait a minute. If Jesus was God in the Flesh and Jesus died, then, in some sense we do need to act as though it was God who died. According to that theology, in the mystery of the cross, God did die. But regardless, any death needs to be mourned because that person who dies is God's child and God mourns for His children, according to the theology of the pastor who chastised us for grieving. So, what was it, really, that prompted his statement? It obviously wasn't theology because he believed what I just wrote above. Later he did mention to us he almost felt guilty that his son was well and we lost ours. Of course, I'll never know his feelings for sure, but I do believe he had unresolved feelings of his own and instead of working through his own hurt and uncertainty, he projected his feelings sideways toward us in our time of grief and loss. For us, at that time, it just made the hurt worse.

What did this teach me on my road to real? If theology **blocks** the grief process, it is the theology that is wrong, not the grief. We are called to be real. Life brings loss and sadness. If we do not grieve, honestly grieve, we will never be fully real. It is important to remember those who have died, to be real, grieve, mourn, and be gentle with our words. More will be said about this in later chapters because my journey to being real is very closely tied to the events of death, loss, grief, and mourning. Come to think of it, this is a common experience all of us share. All of us face death, illness, grief, and suffering. It is truly a part of being real that needs more attention than we are sometimes willing to give.

That confession is truly part of the road to real for us all.

Dark Fear

The evil one would take our power away…
And bolster his power through our reactions.
Fear, anger and worry are fuel for his means.

He feeds off our distresses and upheavals.
Yet… he has neither right nor claim to those emotions.
We are God's child and as such those feelings are His.

As we give them to the "One" we thwart the dark one.
He is diminished and his power and control fade.
He cannot continue the onslaught in the face of God.

We can still be angry or fearful or worried…
It happens to us all…but by claiming God's love…
He keeps us safe under His umbrella …

Gathering in our emotions that have run amuck…
Defuses them and allows us the freedom to re-channel…
And use that energy more appropriately.

Carol A Bond

"I'm Sorry Your Son Died"

We can carry grief and loss around for a long time without even being aware of the load we are bearing. Have you even been really sick and didn't know how sick you were until you began to feel better? It is very much like that when we hang onto the pain of loss, but still live our lives as though nothing is wrong, remaining unaware that we have a part of ourselves blocked off because of the unresolved or complicated grief. When Clay died I did my best to handle it with faith and trust. If I couldn't do that, I just blocked out the feelings and went into my logical and religious self and handled it rationally. Ah, the fallacy of feeling the need to hide our true feelings from ourselves only to find we're alienated from the whole process on that road to being real.

During the year of completing my Bachelor of Arts at Baker University I was busy studying at home while the children were at school and Carol was at work. I was sitting comfortably on our bed on a nice fall day in 1977, reading something I don't remember now. For some reason I was suddenly struck by a wave of memory and emotion from Clay's death eleven years before. I was shocked at the strength of the emotion and found myself saying, out loud, "God my son died!"

Now, memory is a strange thing. I don't remember, now, if I heard an audible voice, or if this all happened in my head. I remember it as an actual conversation, so I will tell it that way. I was shaking physically and emotionally. I wasn't thinking much because I was so immersed in the feelings that there was no room for thought. I heard God (how did I know it was God?) say, "I'm sorry your son died." It wasn't said loudly but rather quietly and with an authentic sadness to it. To say I was surprised would be a bit of an understatement. I really didn't expect an audible answer and even if I had, there was no way my past experience or training would have led me to believe God would apologize for anything. But, I said, in reply, "Thank you." That seems so weird when I think back on it now. But what *do* you say when God apologizes? I am sure I still don't know. I sat there, all nervous and jittery inside. I didn't know what else to say so I just shut up. Then I heard God say, "Will you forgive me for the death of your son?"

I had been a Seventh Day Baptist all my life. I read the Bible. I preached sermons. I led Bible Studies. Nothing like this had ever surfaced before. We ask God for forgiveness. We need to do that because we are sinners. Does that sound familiar? It was just the only way I had been taught. Yet now, God was asking me if I would forgive **Him**? After a pause, I said, "Yes, I forgive you for the death of my son." The funny thing is that I hadn't even been aware I needed to forgive God or that I was even angry with Him at all. We can't be mad at God. It just isn't done! I'm not even supposed to be mad at other people but now, was I really angry at God for the death of my son? Was I blaming God that Clay died? I knew I was angry because my ulcer proved it. Other people knew I had a sharp, cutting manner when they did something I did not approve of. My children and my wife had seen me angry. I punched holes in doors, threw toys across the room and things like that. Oh, you too? Yeah, it seems we all get mad at the people we love the most. But now, did that mean I might love God very much, too, and that was the reason I was mad at Him for Clay's death? And I wasn't even aware of that anger. Go figure.

So, now I told God that I forgave Him. My mind was in a whirl, incomplete thoughts racing around trying to gain my attention but I wasn't able to put them in any kind of order. In the midst of this mental chaos I heard that quiet voice say, "My Son died too." Oh my. Now I am really confused. Yes, I am a Baptist preacher, remember? I know about Jesus dying on the cross, and I know why He did it and I can preach about the crucifixion or the resurrection with the best of them. But, I had never, ever thought about God being the Daddy of His boy who died—just like me! It is interesting that our logical beliefs can block something so basic yet here I was, discovering for the first time that God was a parent who also grieved the loss of a child. He understood. He really, really understood. So, I said, to Almighty God, "I am sorry your Son died." And He said "Thank you."

Then, as though I hadn't had enough revelations for one day, He added, "I forgive you for the death of my Son too." Now, don't go and get too theological now. Stay with me. This wasn't about theology, or doctrine, or dogma, or sacrament. This was about grief and loss. This was about breaking out of more than eleven years of emotional dishonesty and unawareness. I couldn't train to be a chaplain unless I was willing and able to be real. And this, my friends, was about as real as it gets. The journey to real is no picnic. And it wasn't over yet.

Depression

Interesting how easy it is to slip into the blues
Can be as simple as comparing our self to others
Or a word…TV…a book…or being let down
The negative vibes are so quick to adhere
They stick like a magnet holding them tight
It is very difficult to brush them off and see reality

It's easy to vacillate from faith to despair
From hope to the slimy muck of the bog
Sometimes it seems there's a light shining
We feel encouraged and dare to be positive
Only to have the bulb burn out and darkness return
Leaving us riding the roller coaster of fickle emotions

So each day is faced with determination to get through it
Joy and peace seem far away…we go through the motions
Hope lies wallowing in the dust of another disappointment
Vision is clouded with the bombardment of problems
The body is wearied…the mind distraught and at a loss
God, "Give us this day" our daily needs and "Hear our prayers!"

Carol A Bond

"You Can Do That?"

I was a licensed pastor in our Seventh Day Baptist denomination since 1963 when I received my "call" to the ministry and began serving as pastor in 1966. I studied as a biology major in a liberal arts college for two years and as a seminary student for two years at Calvary Bible College. During my bible college training, I pastored a small church in Kansas City for a couple of years. Later, I pastored two churches in Rhode Island full time and filled the pulpit of another church close by. It was during those early years as a young pastor that I learned a very important lesson—not in the classroom but from life.

It so happened that one of those we knew, a single lady, became pregnant. Later we learned her baby died soon after birth. Some felt it was God's judgment on her for having a child out of wedlock. I must admit, at the time, I wondered about that as well. In any case, it was my Christian duty as a pastor to visit this woman in her home to offer spiritual comfort. After all, she was suffering from the usual postpartum depression as well as the grief of losing the life of a child who had been carried close to her heart for nine months. My wife and I lost a child who died at birth, so we had that also as motivation to help if we could. For that reason and because of the entire situation, I felt it prudent to have my wife along during the visit; she, being the good pastor's wife, agreed. In this way, I felt it was safe to visit the lady and not cause any basis for gossip among the church members. I was very aware of how things might look if the young pastor visited a lady of already questionable ethics alone in her home. Such was my mindset at the time.

When my wife and I were invited into the lady's home, she seated herself in a recliner in a corner of the room and curled up in it much like a small child would do. Her eyes were red and swollen from crying, and she was in tears for most if not all of our visit. I sat at a "comfortable distance" from her with my wife seated at my side. I read Scripture, prayed with her, talked about God's love and the need for all of us to be intentional about doing God's will in our lives so we wouldn't have unnecessary problems. I did this for quite some time, but the lady hardly looked at me and kept on crying softly, there in her chair in the corner of the room. I continued to do my pastoral best to walk the line between care and spiritual guidance.

My wife, by training as a nurse and by nature as who she is has strong qualities of compassion and discernment. She spoke up after I had done my "job" as the pastor by reading Scripture, praying, and exhorting to righteousness. What she said is still as vivid in my mind as it was on that day. She said, "Can I ask you a question?" The woman looked up at my wife and said, "Yes." My wife then said the words that are so very important to me, now, as a pastor, chaplain, and counselor.

She said, "It must be very hard for you to believe right now, so until you can believe for yourself again, will you let me believe for you?" The woman looked at my wife and with a glimmer of hope on her face said, "You can do that?" I remember thinking to myself at the same time, "You can do that?" Carol then said she could, and she would be glad to do so if that is what would help her. The lady responded that it would help. After appropriate farewells and goodbyes, we left her and returned to our home. I've never been the same person since that day.

I know what Carol said helped that grieving woman because I could see the change come over her. I also know that what Carol said helped me because I will never be in a similar situation again without thinking of that option in approach and sometimes in actual words spoken. As it happens, during the many years since that time, there have been numerous opportunities to share those words with those who find it difficult to believe because of their loss, grief, and pain.

Those in need of spiritual or emotional care will always tell us what they need—but the message may be in some kind of code. It is our task, as those who care, to break that code and only then to offer the needed help. The woman that day was screaming out in body language, in her chosen place in the room, by her tears, and by her willingness to see the pastor that she was ready to receive spiritual care. I didn't read or understand the code. My wife did. Some would say Carol has the gift of discerning of spirits. I do agree with that but even for those who don't have that particular spiritual gift (I Corinthians 12: 7-10), we can all read body language. We can all observe what is said and done in code and try to break that code to offer what is needed instead of doing what we have been taught or what the rules say we "should" do or say.

And then, there is the matter of not promoting a scandal by visiting someone with "a bad reputation." While that is an appropriate concern to have, it is not the primary concern. I remember Jesus was criticized for being with "the wrong kind" of people when he did his ministry. If we do ministry to those who need it most, there will always be some element of risk. Sometimes it will include physical danger and at other times it will involve reputation risk. While it isn't good practice to be reckless, it is also not good practice to always stay safe.

In my addiction counseling, I see both male and female clients individually, behind closed doors. Trust is essential in any therapeutic encounter. Trust is built upon risk. I cannot expect my clients to trust me if I don't take a certain, appropriate level of risk with them also. They need to feel safe in my presence, and they have a right to expect that kind of safety. If, by my actions, I say to them that I don't trust them, I'm also saying I don't trust myself. In that process, the therapeutic relationship is damaged severely.

==What I learned was to set a trust environment==, often without them even knowing what I was doing. When a discussion veered into the area of being seductive or relationally inappropriate, I would bring into the process my appreciation of the healthy marriage I had with my wife, or what my daughter had taught me about being honest or something else that had its roots in my own satisfying relationships in life. This did two things. It allowed the client to hear healthy boundaries that attracted them to wanting those limits, and it reminded me of what I would lose if I allowed a momentary lapse of relationship consciousness. Actually, I would often be proactive and make this kind of format part of the introductory portion of the session to remind not only the client, but also myself, of the value found in healthy intimacy. This kept us both safe and it did so without being rude or insulting to a client who had already been so badly damaged in this area by others who used, abused, and blamed them. This isn't an unproven theory but an approach that worked with literally hundreds of women and men, whose love lives had been waking nightmares. Their response to my taking a risk invited them to do the same. My willingness to trust myself allowed them to consider trusting themselves. My use of a healthy marriage and family life kept us *all* safe from inappropriate violation of the boundaries that we all need to have in every one of our life experiences.

What my wife did for that woman is a constant source of encouragement to me. We can believe for others who cannot, at the time, believe for themselves. Part of that believing for them, in a clinical setting, is to set healthy boundaries that are inviting of intimacy but also protective of the limits that they can trust. I remember what one of my professors said to me one day many years ago. He was a professor of Bible and also an ordained minister. He told of a time when one of his female parishioners came to him and wanted to have an intimate, physical relationship. He said, "I can be either your lover or your pastor. I cannot be both. I want to be your pastor." There is no blame and no shame in that statement. We can provide a safe place where others can feel cherished, valued, and affirmed without getting any of that confused with making excuses for behaviors that are damaging and inappropriate. We can also do this without being insulting, demeaning, critical, judgmental, or blaming. We can trust ourselves to be who we need to be and in so doing give an invitation that helps them, and ourselves, continue on the road to becoming real.

Relief from Muddled Minds

Sometimes the fog comes down and we can't see the way
The heavy damp cold surrounds us…freezing us into inaction
The icy fingers of fear invade our thinking and hold us captive
Everything appears murky and unclear, we are stymied
At some point the sun rises and the fog begins to fade
The path once more becomes apparent and we can move
Though we may not know which way to go…our vision is clear

Illness, death, mourning, financial worries, job loss are like fog
They muddle our mind and prey on our very soul
Faith, belief and prayer are sorely needed but seem hopeless
The Spirit Person comes in to visit and brings calm and warmth
Easing away the darkness and bringing the Son to their lives
Through the strength of their faith, hope and belief on behalf
of others
The light breaks through and once again they can see the road

Their burdens are eased by sharing them with God's guide

May peace, light, hope and wisdom light the way through
the Spirit

You my dear are the guide…
you open the way…
      light the narrow path…
           break the walls of darkness…
                  shatter the forces of evil…
                        and chase away the fog and cold.

I salute you and others that are guides.

Carol A Bond

Discerning of Spirits

Experiences are matters of perception that make a lasting impression and change our lives. Experiences are profoundly important to the one having them and also very difficult to convey to someone who hasn't had the same or a similar experience. But, for whatever it's worth, the following account is as truthful as anything can be and, even though I still don't understand it well, it actually happened as it is now told. All I do know is that this experience changed my life in profound and beneficial ways.

Carol and I moved to Rhode Island in January 1968 and left there in October 1969. Our stay seemed a lot longer because so much happened during that period of almost two years. We went there to take the pastorate of two small churches about ten miles apart. One church service was in the morning each Sabbath (Saturday) and the other service was in the afternoon at 2:00. Later we supplemented our income by adding another church, which met on Sunday, and I preached there each Sunday morning. In effect, I pastored three churches for almost two years while Carol stayed at home except for the Sabbath services where she played the piano while watching our small children. She did this very well by planning ahead and having Cheerios or something similar for them to munch on as they sat close to her side while she played. The Sunday church congregation had their own pianist. Week after week, we had the same routine where Carol cared for the children and played the piano after supporting her pastor husband in getting services ready. We managed but it was very difficult. Eventually, one of the youth helped Carol with the children at the morning service and was a babysitter for us on a few other occasions. We still keep in close contact with her these many years later since we consider her our "daughter" and she still calls us "mama and papa." Even in the midst of stress, there can often be a welcome relief.

I, as a young pastor, was stretched beyond my meager training and skills. Carol, as a young mother and pastor's wife, was pushed beyond what could be reasonably expected of her as well. Our parsonage was old and cold, the income was barely enough to provide for our needs, and the unresolved grief from one child's death and the serious health problems with our youngest only added to the stress and strain. We tried to keep on keeping on because we believed we had no choice but to do so. We were very duty focused.

It was during this time when some really strange things happened in the parsonage house. I was gone a great deal, doing visitation and services during the weekday evenings and occasionally for a week or two attending required denominational training. Therefore, Carol was often by herself at home with the children. I had the only car and so she was without transportation even if she had wanted to go somewhere. Our TV could pick up a couple of channels, and she and the children watched some things of interest to break up the day. There was little to divert her attention other than the children, home duties, church activities, the garden, and worship preparation. Few visitors came by other than our "other daughter" who brightened our home and played with the children. This wasn't Kansas farm country where folks were just plain neighborly; this was New England, where folks pretty much kept to themselves. It wasn't an easy time for Carol at all.

Now come the strange experiences that actually happened although we didn't know what to do about them. In the late evening after Carol and the children had gone to bed, a snarling wolf appeared to my wife near her head, standing close beside her, facing the end of the bed. He came each time a well-dressed man in a dark suit would appear and stand at the foot of the bed. This happened many times and always when I was gone and away from my family doing church work. Carol was frightened of both figures, the ferocious wolf and the silent, expressionless man and thought she was losing her mind or imagining things. She finally told me and I wasn't sure what to do about it either. I went upstairs and as I was about halfway up the staircase, I felt a sudden and dramatic chill. With it came a sense of pressure. It felt like nothing I had ever experienced before. I was surprised, to say the least, and also frightened. The sensation stayed with me for a few moments and then was gone. I didn't see any wolves or men in dark suits. I felt only the coldness and the pressure. So, now I was really confused. I had no doubt Carol experienced what she reported because she was really scared, or more to the point, terrified.

Not long after that, it stormed with thunder and lightning very close by. I went outside to bring our black Lab dog inside out of his fenced pen because the storm was severe. The dog was frantically climbing the fence, wild-eyed and almost crazy with fear, which wasn't usual for him. He streaked inside and went upstairs to our bedroom where he stayed right there with us as the storm crashed and blew outside. The house shook from the violence of wind and thunder. No rain fell but the wind was fierce.

The next day I visited church members in our small town and commented about the storm the night before. They all looked at me strangely and said, "There wasn't a storm last night." Sure enough, there had been no storm in town or in the area reported on the news. *But, there had been a storm, a bad one, over our house!* The dog knew it, I knew it, and Carol knew it. We decided we lived in a haunted house. And this wasn't a laughing matter. We were genuinely convinced, based on our experiences, something evil was present, and I didn't know what to do about it.

Other strange things occurred, but what happened that night in the "storm" and the recurring image of the snarling wolf and the well-dressed man in a suit who came to stand at the foot of the bed when I was gone continued. Carol couldn't handle it anymore, and I was unable to combat that kind of event so I turned to God and said to Him one day out in the garden, surrounded by trees where nobody could see, "God, if you are so big and powerful, why don't you *do* something!" As difficult as it is to admit I said those words, (at the time I expected to be struck dead for my blasphemy) but I just didn't care anymore. When no lightning came from heaven, it made me even madder so I said, "Okay, God, I quit. I am not going to be a pastor anymore!" We packed a Ryder truck and moved back to Kansas where I went to work at a car dealership. I didn't know what else to do.

The Wolf

The Wolf first came to me
  Many years ago in a turmoil time
Life was hard and we were alone
  To battle the problems and forces
Realization of spirits and their presence
  Was new and fearsome then
Night's dread brought the wolf
  Fierce of face...teeth gleaming

The wolf appeared between me and the man...
  Ready...ferocious ... fangs bared fiercely ...
I knew fear then...yet the man never moved
  He stood...well dressed...eyes cold...unblinking
His very person seemingly very controlled
  Yet no expression on his face of death
These apparitions or spirits came when I was alone
  In the vulnerable twilight of quiet and sleep

Years have passed...those visions gone...yet remain
  Spiritual struggles have prevailed
The wolf came once more...his face only
  He appeared calm...and looked gently at me
Then left and I was saddened and felt lonely
  His beauty and strength of spirit remained
Somehow I knew I was safe when he was there
  Though wild...he was a spirit being

Again he came this time embodied to our campsite
  He placed his front paws on the steps
I saw him as he looked into the camper...
  Slight fear, awe, respect and wonder filled me
Then I saw his great body as he stood there
  Waiting...then he turned and walked away
I could see him looking back inviting me to come
  Other smaller wolves were crowded around him

He the alpha male turned and walked slowly
  Up the grassy slope to the top...hesitated and was gone
I felt alone like I had missed something...but...I couldn't go
  I wondered what would have happened if I had followed
The vision was so clear I can see the scene yet
  In the morning light we checked to see if we saw paw prints
And were disappointed that we could not see any there
  Though knowing it happened only in my mind's eye

He comes when needed; silent...only his countenance speaks
  He wasn't there in the dirt devil that swirled round me in the crowd
He was not visible in the terrible electrical storm
  That crashed and exploded 'round our house
He came in the silence of the night terrors and quiet of early morn
  When the mind was vulnerable and open to see
Now he waits patiently in the wings of the stage
  Ready to protect and keep the dangerous spirits at bay

Carol A Bond

"What Can I Do For You?"

In the spring of 1981, I was in my first clinical unit of CPE (Clinical Pastoral Education) during my last year at Candler School of Theology, Emory University, Atlanta, Georgia. I was one of eight first-quarter students at Grady Hospital, which is a large, 1,200-bed teaching hospital. There were also about the same number of advanced CPE students in supervisory training and in charge of our progress. Basic student chaplains shared on-call duties every eight days at which time we were on duty for twenty-four hours, staying in the hospital for that entire period. Sometimes we had time to sleep in a provided area but always with our pagers by the bedside. The few times we slept, we did so fully clothed. Grady was a busy facility and served as the trauma center, rape receiving center, and general hospital for the entire area. It was always busy. In addition to emergency call, we had regular floors during the day and handled pastoral needs that came up on our respective units.

I listened carefully to the instructions given by the more experienced chaplain interns and tried my utmost to be the best chaplain possible. One thing I heard repeatedly was to be sure and be close to the patient whenever possible and not to stay too far away. As I made my rounds on this particular day, I entered the room of a man in his 50s who was a post-surgery patient, hooked up to many tubes and lines and looking very miserable. I went over close to his bed after he saw me and asked in my best pastoral voice, "Is there anything I can do for you?" His answer was clear as he said, "Yes, you can get off of my catheter!"

Those words ring in my ears yet to this day. From that time on, I was careful to look where my feet were and to be on the alert for tubes, wires, lines, or anything else that might be there. Sometimes the best pastoral care is as simple as paying attention to what is going on from a very practical standpoint.

I learned to pay attention to what was going on with my patients. Often that alerted me to connections with spiritual issues I might have been missed if I'd an agenda of always reading the Bible or praying. Sometimes I peeled and sectioned an orange for a patient who couldn't do it. At times, it was getting ice for the water pitcher (making sure first that the patient was allowed to have more fluids.) I paid attention to the physical environment, but I was also careful to act within my job description and not cross over into the medical area of care. There was no clear boundary but nurses told me they didn't appreciate visitors who crossed that line. I was the chaplain. I didn't do medical care, or even limited physical care, until I checked with the nurse.

My patients taught me a great deal even in my desire to be a "good chaplain," which did at times backfire. In a particularly well remembered situation, one of my patients was a young man who had been shot six times with a .22 caliber revolver by his girlfriend. Evidently she was mad enough to empty the gun into his body. When he came into the hospital, the bullets were still inside him and serious infection set in, making surgery risky until the pockets of infection could be treated with antibiotics. He was a very sick young man, not likely to die but would be in critical condition for some time. I went in to visit him, and as I heard from my supervisors, I avoided being too cheery and upbeat. Probably I was a bit too somber because as I quietly came to him, I said in a very calm voice, "Hello, I'm the chaplain," hoping my quiet demeanor would be a comfort to him in his anxiety. Instead of the expected response, his eyes widened and in a shocked voice he said, "Oh, my God, the chaplain's here—am I going to die!?" My good intentions, once again, didn't work out very well. I didn't step on his catheter, paying attention to the physical situation, but I still missed something. Mercy—this chaplain work is more complex than I thought it would be. Visiting people of my church or my family or someone known to me was very different than visiting a complete stranger who had no idea who or what I might be. So, I learned again.

There are books that tell how to visit those in a hospital or other places of care. They are helpful at times, but what I learned and what I was taught by my patients was there is no one size fits all answer to "how to" do visitation. Often, when called to the ER in an emergency situation, I would be asked to be with the terrified family. I needed to let them know who I was because they needed that information and that required me to say I was the chaplain. Before they could totally respond in shock, I would say something like, "I am not here for any bad news, I'm part of the care team and I came to see how you're doing." Usually the family's anxiety would be brief, and they accepted my presence as exactly what it was. I was part of the team and was there for them. Usually I would offer coffee, water, or something and go get that. I gave them time to adjust to having a "chaplain" around because often a chaplain is perceived as support for death. Once the relationship was established, so that when the bad news came, if it did, I was already on board as a person, not just as the bearer of bad news. My patients taught me a lot. I learned not to step on catheters, and I learned to avoid shocking sick patients by saying "I am the chaplain."

It is a high honor to be invited into the trauma and grief of another human being. I never had the "right" to be with a family, regardless of my job description. They had the right to refuse my presence or they could invite me into their life at that time. Very seldom was I refused access but there were times when it took a while to gain a measure of trust. In every case, I paid attention to what was going on around me and around the patient or the family. I learned it pays to be very aware of the answer when I asked, "What can I do for you?"

Be Real

Robert Fulghum says: "The eye that looks in on us
and the eye that looks out from us is not the same eye".
>	(From: <u>Uh-Oh; Some Observations From Both Sides of
>	the Refrigerator Door</u>, p.242)

It's very difficult to Be all we can Be…
Or to be real and in touch with who we really are…
For often we don't know who we are at all…
So how can we Be and be in life and do good?

We seem to create our own self…our own persona…
And we perform and tell it so well we begin to believe it…
We are fabulous actors and tale tellers as we go…
We share here, fill in some there, cover up yonder…

And on it goes until one day we stop and wonder…
Who am I really???? Where do I go from here???
We've forgotten our roots…we are earth, sky and life…
We are energy, power, love and the creation of the "One".

We don't have to act out…we can just be who we are…
If we are willing to get back to basics and find our joy…
And seek out and listen for the Spirit power to touch us…
Then maybe we can have balance, honesty and realness…

Achieving a true balance between the mundane and the holy…

And between the worst that we can be and the best we might become.

Carol A Bond

Breaking Rules

It was my third year of seminary training toward my master's in pastoral care and counseling. I had been challenged in the classroom and in various placements as an intern, including the Atlanta City Prison and a nursing home. Now, I was taking a formal quarter of CPE at Grady Hospital. The hospital administration agreed to call us for any situation where we could provide ministry thereby learning how to do ministry even better. We wrote up some of our visits as verbatims and presented them in a group setting where our work was discussed and challenged. It was a painful but helpful way to learn what we were doing as seen through the eyes of our peers and supervisors. We basic interns shared being on call for twenty-four-hour periods, meaning that once every eight days we didn't go home in the evening but stayed in the hospital, available for the inevitable emergency situations during the night when we were the only chaplain present.

On one particular night on call, I experienced ten emergency calls, six of which were deaths. I was emotionally and physically exhausted and looked forward to 8:00 when the other fifteen chaplain interns arrived and I could go home. At 7:45, the pager went off requesting a chaplain come and baptize a dying infant. One of my peers was an Episcopalian, familiar with infant baptism so he volunteered to cover that call for me. He knew that I, as a Baptist, didn't practice infant baptism. However, I have a very strong work ethic and since I was still officially on duty, I said I'd cover the call. As I went to the elevator I began to realize I was being foolish, and was even going against the theology of my church that taught immersion as the only authentic form of baptism. As the elevator doors closed, I began to panic and became upset. Fortunately, nobody else was on the elevator with me to see my obvious distress. I wanted to provide ministry to this mother whose child was dying, but in order to do that I would have to break some of the rules of my faith. The elevator moved toward the pediatric floor, and I had a sudden moment of crisis in which I struggled inwardly with years of training and programming. But then I had a moment of clarity and peace that felt as if a weight was being lifted from me.

The doors of the elevator opened and I walked to the patient's room to meet the nurse in charge. She informed me that I needed to gown, mask, and glove because of the isolation situation. By the time I donned all the required coverings, I no longer looked like a chaplain. I didn't look like anyone because only my eyes showed. But, inside, I felt like a chaplain. I was not doing chaplaincy—I was being a chaplain. I was a minister who could provide spiritual care to anyone of any faith because all persons are children of God. The rules weren't as important as the need.

So when the nurse said, "Chaplain, what do you need?" I was able to say, "I need some sterile water." I guess my thought was that sterile water made sense for a baptism or maybe I thought it was close to holy water. In any case, the nurse got the water and I took the Bible I always carried and found the passage where Jesus blessed the children. (Mark 10:13-16) As Jason's mother held his tiny body in her arms, I read from Scripture and took some of the water and placed it on Jason's head, baptizing him in the Name of the Father and of the Son and of the Holy Spirit and in the Name of

Jesus. Jason's mother cried, the nurse cried, and so did the chaplain shed tears as well. After visiting with the mother and saying thank you to the nurse, I took off the isolation garb, threw it in the trash, and went home. I learned the next day that Jason died soon after the baptism.

So, here I was, a Seventh Day Baptist pastor from Kansas, baptizing a Baptist mother's child in Atlanta, Georgia. But from that day until the present, I knew the difference between "doing" chaplaincy and "being" a chaplain. A dying child and a grieving mother take precedence over theological rules every time.

By definition, "theology" is the study of God. Theology can be wrong, it can be incomplete, and it can be confusing. There is nothing automatically wrong about having a particular theology unless one is so rigid that the possibility of a different theology is nonexistent or threatening. But what do we do about the "rules" of our faith? If we are Jewish, do we eat pork when it is served at a meal? If we are Amish, do we listen to a TV or radio to participate in our child's graduation from college far away? Some churches don't allow piano playing in church so can members attend a church that has a piano? Some Christians observe the Old Testament feast days and refuse to participate in Christmas. Can these Christians accept a present at Christmas? Native Americans stay with the body of the deceased and accompany it to the funeral home. Do hospital officials block that because of a "policy"? Jehovah Witnesses don't accept blood transfusions. Does the medical staff do a transfusion anyway in order to save a life? Muslims want burial of their dead within twenty-four hours. Does someone hold the body longer because of some technicality? And the list goes on. Beliefs and theologies are important to people of faith. So, why did I violate the clear teachings of my faith and break the rules about baptism?

Years later I worked in a Catholic hospital in Kansas. One day on duty, I was paged by the nursing staff to the operating room. There was an early-stage miscarriage and the family wanted the "baby" baptized. This was a very early pregnancy so there wasn't a fully developed fetus to baptize, which of course made the request difficult for some to understand. The family believed life began at conception, so this was a human being, and the nurses and I respected that. Additionally, this wasn't just infant baptism, which is outside my Baptist theology, but also baptism of a dead body, which goes against Roman Catholic theology. With the family and the nurse present, I had a baptism service for this baby. To some observers it might not have appeared to be a "real" baptism. To the family, I provided a sacrament of love and faith for their loved one. Later I was asked by my Catholic supervisor why I did that when it broke all the rules. My reply was, "It was ministry and comfort to the family." My supervisor accepted that. I do not *do* chaplaincy. I am a chaplain.

Over 3,000 years ago a man named Moses met God in the form of a burning bush on a mountainside in Arabia. Moses, being an inquisitive and intelligent man, asked which god it was because there were many. When asked what God's Name was, God replied, "I am that I am," or as my Hebrew professor said, it can be translated as "I will be whatever you need me to be." Either way, God didn't say "I do what I do." As a pastor who was a chaplain in training, I moved from doing to being that day with Jason. I have never regretted that move at all.

Breaking rules is dangerous. We are totally responsible for that decision and don't have any backup authority to keep us safe. Will I break rules for the sake of a greater need? Yes, sometimes I will—but not always. Once I broke speed laws rushing a worker with battery acid in his eyes to the hospital. I very seldom drive over the speed limit in my driving, even when I am "late." It is a choice. It is my choice.

I remember one class at Emory in which we discussed the ethics of moral living. Usually, most people think of the highest morality person as "the law-abiding citizen." Dr. James Fowler challenged that and said there might be a higher standard to which we are called as Believers in Jesus. Actually, I obey most laws and rules because they keep me safe and contribute to the safety of us all. I like rules and laws. But there do come times when we need to choose between doing what is seen as "right" in the eyes of the community and being "right" according to our own beliefs and the needs of others.

As a closing thought, even Jesus went against some of the "rules" and "laws" of his time and place during his ministry. At least two of his disciples carried concealed weapons in defiance of the Roman law prohibiting Jews from being armed. Jesus broke the Sabbath laws when he healed on that holy day or commanded the one healed to carry his bed after being healed. Dietrich Bonhoeffer, a Lutheran pastor, participated in the plot to assassinate Adolph Hitler and was himself killed by the Nazis for that violation of the laws of the German government. My feeling is that we need to avoid the safety of doing what others say is "right" and act in ways obedient to what might be a higher law. It is a dangerous path but, as my wife and I discovered during our journeys in the mountains of Colorado, sometimes dangerous paths lead to rewarding places.

Truth

Your quest for truth is taking you down dark path ways
Filled with questions, disillusionment and maybe fear
The shackles of loyalty to the past begin to break loose
Voices from church, leaders and parents fade into whispers

The path is treacherous, strewn with rocks, ruts and vines
The old teachings no longer hold true to life and experience
Even the Bible seems contradictory and generates questions

You proceed through the gray mists of difficulty and vagueness
All the while cataloging what you know from working with others
Processing teachings, beliefs, prayer and how they affect outcomes
Stepping carefully through the roadblocks sorting truth from wishes

Going back in time seeking the accuracy of the Bible as it was written
Ever searching for the elusive reality through the shadowy forest
Carry on hunter--that for which you seek is near--do not be diverted.

Carol A Bond

Explosions

I was a chaplain intern at Grady Hospital in Atlanta in spring 1981, during a time of racial unrest due to the child murders going on in that city. Nobody knew why black children were being killed, and some believed it was the ugly remnants of racism rearing its hateful head. The sixteen chaplaincy students and many pastors were called to the hospital because of an explosion in a daycare center. All of the children were black and few, if any, survived the blast. Parents were summoned to come to the morgue to identify their children, which, as you may imagine was extremely difficult for everyone involved. The more experienced, advanced students were present with families at the morgue and those of us who were basic students were assigned to many waiting rooms where families gathered. All the families were black. I was very white and talked with a northern accent. I wasn't one of them at all, and they knew it. Several times local pastors came in to talk with their parishioners so I functioned as a messenger getting information, water, coffee, or other needed items. I also visited with some families, but the reception was understandably suspicious, cool, and distant. Everyone suspected the explosion was a bomb set off by a white hate group. It turned out later after investigation that a boiler exploded, not a bomb. It was a terrible accident, not a racist hate episode. There was much grief, crying, and sometimes just sullen depression. It wasn't a pleasant room as family members came from the morgue and others waited to go to the morgue.

Eventually, a man came into the room, talking with families in quiet tones and writing notes down in his tablet. I noticed he didn't have an official hospital nametag so I went to him and asked who he was. He told me that I didn't need to know and he had every right to be there. Now, that didn't go over well with me at all. I was thirty-eight years old, in my prime, very fit, and was working part time as a night security guard downtown to help with our limited income. I didn't appreciate his attitude. I felt responsible for these grieving families, and I felt protective. I demanded to know who he was. He informed me he was a reporter for some New York newspaper, and he had the right of the press to interview these people.

By now, everyone in the room could hear our conversation and when I told him he had to leave because these families didn't need him to interrogate them at this time, they were paying attention to these two white guys going at it. He said I couldn't make him leave. That was a big mistake. I pushed him out the door with his heels digging into the carpet, bouncing defiantly along but I shoved him out the door anyway and said not to come back. He threatened but I told him to stay away. Then I went back and sat down. After that, the families warmed up to me and we talked, prayed, cried, and worked together on their grief. To this day, I don't know who that reporter was but I suspect God might have somehow been involved. That interaction opened up my opportunity to minister to the families. My addicts that I work with now would call that "A God Thing." Maybe it was.

As this difficult day wore on, there was finally only one young man in the room besides myself. I had visited with him enough to know his baby had died in the explosion. He was devastated, all alone, head down, nobody else there with him. It came time for me to leave and as I walked past him, he looked up, recognized me, and nodded his head in greeting. I stood by him with my hand on his shoulder and said what is probably my best pastoral care of all time. Are you ready for this? I said, "Hey man—I'm sorry." He gave a little sob, glanced at me, grasped my hand and said "Thank you." I left. It was a very difficult day for me and for my fellow chaplains, but it was a horrible day for the families who were there.

"Hey man—I'm sorry" doesn't sound very theological or religious. It isn't profound. It isn't Scriptural. But I still maintain that it is the very best work I have ever done. We had spent hours together. I had stood up for him and his fellow victims of this explosion and had run an intruder out of the room. He trusted me. He believed me. We cried together. Even though he didn't know it, we were both fathers who lost children and it made a connection. To this day, and largely because of that day, I trust the moment to give us the words we need to share with a person who is in deep grief. Instead of falling back onto an easy, familiar, learned response, I listened to him and I talked with him as one human being to another—as one father to another. It was all in a context of faith and we did some religious talk, but the power of the time together was summarized in that one statement. Those were not recited words. Those were torn out of my heart and shared with him.

In our debriefing the next day, my supervisor asked me who I was in that room. He asked if I was a chaplain or a security guard. Good question. Now, I would say the answer is "Yes." I used what I knew and what I did and who I was as I ministered in that room. I did what was needed. Sometimes ministry is getting a glass of cold water, or a cup of hot coffee, or showing someone where the bathroom is. That day, part of my ministry was using my physical strength to bounce an intruder out of a room and to be convincing enough that he didn't even try to come back. He believed me. I believed me, too, and so did the families in that room.

Explosions—they come in many forms. Sometimes they are destructive like that boiler explosion that killed scores of children and tore families apart. Sometimes, explosions are those of our behavior that can be just as violent and most certainly as strong. My primary supervisor at Emory said one day, "Sometimes the nicest thing you can do for somebody is the not nice thing." Sometimes we need an explosion. Sometimes we need to do the not nice thing. I believe this was such a day and even though I wondered at the time of the debriefing if I had done the "right" thing with that reporter, I am sure now. God used who I was and what I did to provide what was needed at that time. What I believe now is that we don't always have to be tough—but we do always need to be real.

Believe

Why do things happen the way they do?
Why does it seem we're so often thwarted?
Why does it feel we're singled out for trouble sometimes?
Why does it seem that a Power greater…isn't there?
Why does our faith rise and ebb like the tides?
Why do we believe at all…is it only because of a book?
Why do we need something greater than ourselves?

It would seem that "stuff" happens…you fall, you get hurt
Our decisions, our health, our attitude all play a part.
Natural occurrences…tornadoes and floods take place
The world is no longer perfect …
Disease, suffering and illness come due to that brokenness
Or arise due to life's natural ensuing processes
Wars, abuses, people hurting other people come from choices

These decisions can be appropriate or bring disaster and pain.
The evil spirit is real…yet "God" does not stop all unpleasantness
"Bad" things are allowed …for His purpose or plan we do not know
We are given freedom to live or die…with or without faith
Why there is intervention one time and not another…
Or why innocents suffer…remains the eternal mystery
All we see is the *now* happening…not the whys and wherefores.

The Book that tells of Creator, life, death, hope, faith, Savior and eternity…
Records that even Job in his close relationship did not know why.
Where does that leave us in our daily life of dealing with the ups and downs?
Again…it boils down to choice…
Do we eat of the apple of skepticism…or partake of the manna of hope?
We are all incomplete… that's why we need each other…
We know inside we are missing a part of us…which is relationship…

"God" is a part of that empty space…we seek Him/Her always.

Carol A Bond

"I Have Nothing to Say"

During my intern year after my formal training at Emory, to be a chaplain, I worked with the alcohol and drug treatment unit at the Kansas City hospital where my advanced clinical pastoral education occurred. I was allowed to be part of the treatment experience and was quite interested in the process of working with people whose lives had been severely damaged by alcohol and drug abuse. Many of them were really quite likable and were, in fact, much like me. Anyway, the counselors gave a community workshop on alcohol/drug treatment and since I was the chaplain, I was asked to give a talk on "spirituality" in recovery. Preparing for this, I realized I really had nothing to give. I had a master's in theology, pastoral care, and ethics, but I had little to say about spirituality. It was really quite troubling, and I told the counselors I had nothing to say. They gave a presentation and basically said spirituality was really love and explained that to the audience. Not bad. Not bad at all. But the fact remained: ***I didn't know what spirituality meant to me apart from religion.***

I had to discover if spirituality was indeed something different or if all spirituality had to be linked somehow to a religious experience. Remember, I said in the previous paragraph that many of the addicted patients were a lot like me? I was told in Atlanta that I had an alcoholic personality. If you know any Baptist preachers, I would suggest this isn't something they want to hear. I certainly didn't. So, the real reason I was there at that hospital, in the setting of a recovery unit was that I wanted to prove that supervisor wrong. I wasn't sure what an "alcoholic personality" was, but I was very sure I didn't have one. I was halfway through my year at Bethany and had begun to realize my story was very similar to my clients' and my behaviors and feelings were virtually identical, as well. This finally brought me to the realization the Atlanta supervisor was right. What did that mean? I had never been drunk, and I had never used illegal drugs. But, I had used prescription valium for a number of months back in 1971 because of my anger that caused a bleeding ulcer. I came to realize that it isn't what is used, how much is used, or the source of what is used but the effect on the individual that determines addiction. As I began to examine myself, I was drawn to the Twelve Step program I'd been teaching to others and began to apply it to myself.

It fit. Not only that, as they say in AA, "It works if you work it." So, I began to work the Twelve Step program for myself. I found it fit in perfectly with my Baptist theology and my biblical heritage. It had to do with behaviors more than belief, but that was fine with me because what we do is a better marker for faith than what we say we believe.

I struggled a bit as I tried to define for others what I was discovering for myself, but gradually a definition began to emerge. I shared with my patients and my peers. I honed and refined what I presented until it began to make sense to others, not only to me. As is my usual pattern, I started with a quite complicated definition until I finally whittled it down to where it was more simple and workable. As my career became more stable, I had the opportunity to share with clients in an inpatient, twenty-eight day program in Topeka, Kansas. Here, I met with the patients on a daily basis, several times each day, and we shared back and forth what it meant to be a spiritual person and ways to work a spiritual program. This didn't prevent or block working a religious program if that was desired, but it wasn't the same as religion either. I could share what I believed when asked but also was free to present spiritual options and help patients find ways to express their own discoveries that fit them at that time. "At that time" became the key concept because each person's journey was a bit different. I learned to trust that the Higher Power would guide each person on his or her path, not according to what I thought or using the words that I used but what was best for each person according to the Higher Power's plan for their lives. It actually worked quite well. It also helped me with my growth in humility and trust. Anyone who claims to be an expert in spirituality shows by that statement they haven't quite figured it out, as that's not the goal. However, progress was made toward that end.

If I am asked now to talk about spirituality I feel confident in doing so, and I find that people who have had a less than positive experience with church can begin to claim their spiritual relationship in healthy ways. But I remember how all this came about. I had to admit that I really had nothing to say. I did not bluff my way through to save face. I just admitted my lack of ability and went from there. This brings us to what we discovered out of that whole process.

Spirituality is about behaviors that come from and reflect what we really believe. There are five behaviors that we distilled from nine markers for addiction found in an early version of the DSM IIIR back in 1984. We used those five behavioral markers as the basis for my spiritual assessments and also for clinical notes when describing for the care team a patient's spiritual progress. Things like prayer, belief in God, reading the Bible, attending church, and similar observations are often used to determine a level of spirituality.

We didn't go there. Our five markers were: honesty, risk, trust, humility, and gratitude. Each of these is measured against self, others, and God (Higher Power.) Many religious people would fail this kind of spiritual test. Ideally, spirituality and religion will work together, but if we look at history, including the Bible, we see they often do not. Religious fanaticism has resulted many times in the absence of these five markers. So, we worked on a behavioral model of spirituality and sometimes clients would use them in their church/religious life also with good results.

Interestingly, these five markers work well in assessing how healthy any relationship, including a marriage relationship, is also. A marriage without honesty, risk, trust, humility and gratitude is not a relationship at all and is in fact already a divorce waiting to happen. So, what began as an admission of failure became a very useful process of discovery which helped many recovering clients through the years. These markers have also been used in couple's counseling and workshops for healthcare professionals in hospitals, nursing homes and other places where spirituality is a goal. When I attended a seminar in 2002 presented by George Washington University I found that they came up with a description of spirituality in the training of their physicians that used the same markers. Just as important, I have come to trust that there is a Spiritual Power that can and does restore us to sanity. And this included me. What a concept.

Balance

We cannot live in a world with no **anger**
Though it's hard to face when it's directed at us
Anger shows we are alive, we care and have ideas

We cannot live in a world with no **change**
Though frustrating nothing remains constant or we'd stagnate
Thus we have opportunity to experience and become more

We cannot live in a world with no **craziness**
Though we may not know it we are all a bit touched
Logic to lunacy is human and our goal is wholeness

We cannot live in a world with no **criticism**
Though it's tough to take no matter how constructive
Yet trust, risk and openness are positive invitations to develop

We cannot live in a world with no **differences**
Though it can be challenging it helps to complete us
For variety, contrast, love and diversity in life are invigorating

We cannot live in a world with no **failure**
Though we shudder at the thought…it is "normal"
This does not mean we are failures, only that we're free to grow

We cannot live in a world with no **feelings**
Though we negate them and deny the sadness, fear, love and pain
Without them we are not honest or in touch with ourselves or others

We cannot live in a world with no **love**
Though we may not realize how much we need affection to truly live
It keeps us centered in confidence, empathy, faith, hope and joy

We cannot live in a world with no **stress**
Though we'd like it otherwise…today's world is pressure filled
But tension helps us function and to stretch to new heights

We cannot live in a world with no **weakness**
Though we want perfection we all have some frailty
And vulnerability, honesty and sensitivity build strength

Carol A Bond

Spirituality

In the previous chapter we explored the process of how I came to understand spirituality. Here, we will look at it more closely and determine why it is important to develop it as something separate from religion. A large part of my own personal journey to being "real" is the process of learning the difference between being spiritual and being religious. I am a religious person, identified as such by my education, my experience, my ordination as a minister, and my profession as a chaplain. Whether or not I am also a *spiritual* person, however, cannot be identified quite so easily. In our Christian Bible, we read that Jesus made a clear distinction between the two concepts. In effect, he was a religious person who was also primarily, deeply spiritual. His disputes with other "religious" persons were often around their lack of authentic spirituality. He saw the difference. The religious people of his day did not. Not much has changed in that area during the two thousand years since.

On the medical floors of the hospital where I worked, the chaplains all charted in the patient's chart in the progress notes along with other disciplines. So while I wasn't a stranger to that process, now I was expected to be part of the treatment plan for each substance abuse patient. Using the five spiritual behaviors described in the previous chapter as indicators for a person's spiritual distress or strength worked very well and interfaced with other entries. Specific religious orientations were not the issue. Spirituality was. Identifying issues of honesty, risk, trust, humility, and gratitude became useful in the entire care plan for all patients, not only those with addiction.

During my years working with addicted clients, we, as a staff, would sometimes use the spiritual assessment as the primary access into a patient's emotional and psychological difficulties. We found on that unit and also on the cancer floor that "everything is connected." A person's attitude, diet, disease, family, beliefs, history, hopes, fears, and everything else, all affected everything else. Our opportunity became a matter of using any access point we could find to get to the root of the addiction problem or the stress of cancer treatment, no matter what it might be. Spiritual assessment made sense.

But there was still the matter of disentangling the spiritual from the religious, especially for those clients who had experienced a toxic faith or a shaming religious history. Since a person's concept of God is often based upon an experience of parenting, usually by a father, it became a matter of unlearning before a healthy spiritual life could be established. My clients helped me with this as they gave feedback, often strongly or even profanely, about what they did or did not believe. They taught me that if one wanted to understand all human behavior, it is helpful to study addiction. Defects of character are shared by all human beings but in addiction, they become so magnified that they become easier to observe. If one takes that exaggerated and obvious understanding and uses that as a diagnostic microscope, the defects in all other persons become more observable. All of us have grandiosity to some extent. Addicts take that to an extreme. Low self-worth plagues us all at times, but it devastates the addict or alcoholic. The study of addiction, when the recovering addict is willing to be honest and to trust, can open up a useful access point to anyone who wants to help people in emotional or psychological crisis. I learned to trust that and to go to what I learned from my clients when I needed help understanding how it all fit together. Questions about whether a person could remain an agnostic and still work a spiritual program, or how a Native American can maintain his or her traditional practices and be in an equal standing, spiritually, with someone who professes to be a Christian were the easy questions. Much more difficult ones were asked, and we worked on these and found spiritual answers that fit into healthy religious practices but which were also not dependent upon them.

I came to be convinced that a spiritual person is not always religious and that a religious person is not always spiritual. Many evils have been done in the name of religion. It doesn't take much research to discover that. The Spanish Inquisition and the KKK are only two obvious examples. The "HOW" of recovery (honesty, openness, willingness) dovetailed very well with the teachings of Jesus. Honesty, risk, trust, humility, and gratitude fit well with what it takes to build a healthy worship practice. In an ideal world, all religious people are also deeply spiritual, and spiritual people will find a way to express their beliefs and behaviors with others who believe the same. But then, the old enemy of spirituality would crop up and someone would say, "But, that is not the RIGHT way to believe." My answers to that varied from "being right is not all it's cracked up to be" to "we are all wrong about some things anyway" to "I would be glad to join the one true church if only I knew which to join of the many who claim to be the one." So many groups claim they are "right" and yet behave so "wrong" through the practice of hate, intolerance, shame, and low self-worth. Based on the feedback from clients and their family members, I came to believe that "no fault, no blame, no excuse" was the only way to work a truly spiritual program. I began to see that the teachings of

Jesus, although sometimes interpreted through religious rhetoric, present the same truth.

"Who sinned—this man or his parents?" (John 9:2, NIV) was asked two thousand years ago and the answer needs to remain the same. It is not a matter of fault or blame. The spiritual answer is to be responsible for what we ourselves do or do not do when confronted with the problems in life. So often, perhaps more often in addiction, the question of "whose fault is it?" comes up. Who is to blame? Who, then, can be excused? Spirituality doesn't need to know because the spiritual person knows who is responsible. We are each responsible for our own decisions and choices, regardless of our childhood or other problems in our life. There is no excuse, but neither is there room for blame and fault. Those are dead-end roads.

"Working a spiritual program" is a common phrase in addiction recovery. The concept is not unknown in church or religious circles either. However, spelling that out into a practical pattern of behavior is not quite so easily done. The people I consider to be most real are people who practice the five behaviors in every area of their lives. Relationships that are healthy are relationships that practice the same five behaviors. I don't believe a person can be spiritual without them. Of course there are other markers for spirituality such as patience, love, diligence, faith, and so on.

But on my road to real, I found a spiritual program is possible, beneficial, and also observable. Addicts and alcoholics can sometimes be very blunt. In many ways and often at just the right time, they reminded me they weren't the only ones needing to practice the five spiritual behaviors. They challenged me to exercise the same process in my own life. Perhaps that was the greatest benefit to me. I was not an expert in working a spiritual program. A spiritual program calls everyone to become more than we are. It can be documented without condemning the person who has failed to develop one or more of those behaviors. But when all five work together and interrelate in a healthy fashion, truly miraculous things happen. Serenity happens. Joy happens. Peace happens. Relationships flourish. And we become more real. And that, still, is my goal.

But wait—there's still more! One time when I was on vacation, one of the local pastors volunteered to cover my groups for me while I was gone. When I returned, the patient group had a question they wanted to ask. It seems this good pastor told them they were not spiritual persons, and they needed to become spiritual before they could recover from addiction. We discussed that in quite some detail and what I told the group was that they were already spiritual persons but had, in their addictions, become involved with the wrong spirit. They now were finding a much better one. Not everyone is sensitive enough to their wrongs that they are willing to admit the exact nature of those wrongs to God, self, and another human being. Most of those I worked with in recovery were that open and honest. How many "good" people not in addiction are willing to take such a close look at their defects? Someone doesn't need to be an addict to be honest about their faults, but it helps to feel a need for change. Spiritual people are open to change.

As a result, I became more careful in screening coverage for my groups when I was going to be gone. One of my good friends was a Catholic Sister who covered several times for me. The clients loved her. She knew the difference between religion and spirituality. Her love, compassion, and practical view of life won my addicts over. I was pleased to have her substitute for me because she was another person from whom I learned much on my own road to real—and to spirituality.

Addiction

An addiction is an overwhelming action of doing that which a person
Feels driven to do, be it drinking, drugging, eating, sex or whatever
Just merely deciding not to do that particular thing does not work
The spirit of addiction is strong and not easily relinquished
The draw for some is camaraderie with others in the usage of substances
For some it's the release of stress, worry, inferior feelings, fear
Or a way to forget the past, present or even the future
As it numbs, it provides bravado, or "feel good" feelings even though
More and more is required to meet the pull of the ever seductive desire

The past may have been full of all kinds of experiences
From abandonment, abuse and neglect to normal and caring
It is up to each one how to utilize those lessons for good or not
The past cannot be changed… it is gone…it is today that is available
Life's lessons can be utilized for growth, forgiving, building
Or to use as an excuse to escape from responsibilities and making choices
Addiction stalls the growing up process and delays fulfilling one's destiny
It keeps most from feelings, from relationship, from honesty and
From developing faith, impairs the perspective and limits trust

Coming to grips with the past, letting go while not excusing
Those that have harmed …or embracing those who gave love
Is foremost in healing from addictions and self destructive behavior
Accepting the present…seeing the need to evaluate one's own direction
Selecting wiser values, setting priorities, developing faith in God and others
While looking to the future with hope as amends are made…
Forgiving the past, forgiving self and even forgiving God
Allows a base for shucking guilt, regret, shame, blame and anger
When that enlightenment comes together…life begins anew!

Carol A Bond

"Thank You Jesus!"

Nineteen eighty-three was a really difficult year for our family. We moved back to Kansas in 1981 after completing my training in Atlanta. We bought a house at the then existing interest rate of fifteen percent, Carol had a job as a nurse in a small hospital, and I had a job as counselor on an addiction treatment unit. We were surviving, although with difficulty, along with our three teens, now in high school. At least we were back with family and in our home church.

Then Carol's job went away. Soon after, I lost my job as well. The economy in general wasn't good, and our economy was really not good! During our search for new employment, we did take family time that summer to do inexpensive things with our children and to pick up some money by putting up hay bales for area farmers or by me filling the pulpit for area churches. But it was still very bleak, financially. What had seemed so promising after the five years of training appeared to be smoke and mirrors.

That fall, Carol began working for the State of Kansas, reviewing nursing homes in partnership with a social worker. I found a job as a service writer at a car dealership in Lawrence, Kansas, about twenty-five miles from our home. Finally we were at least able to keep afloat financially, although the past several months put us into a negative cash flow condition. I did good work at the dealership, and Carol was able to use her nursing license and skill to help nursing home staff give proper care to their residents. She traveled many miles but was kept safe on the highways by the grace of God, for which I was grateful.

One day at the dealership, a car drove into the service bay and I went to talk with the driver. My supervisor, the service manager, motioned for me to not take her as a customer because the car was bought at another dealership. Our place of business had the reputation of being the best service facility in the area, and so some folks saved a few miles of travel, or a few dollars of purchase price, at another dealership, but brought it in to us for service under warranty. It made taking care of our own customers more difficult. But I had been the service manager of another dealership years before, and we had built the same kind of reputation. Our customers trusted us and we used that trust to win customers over from other dealers so they purchased new or used vehicles from us in the future. It was a policy that worked well.

So, I asked this lady how I could help her. She looked at me and said, "I am Sister_____ (her name) and I am very worried about my car. I don't know if it is safe to drive on into Topeka." Our dealership was in Lawrence, Kansas, which is roughly halfway between Kansas City and Topeka. I told her I would go on a test drive with her to diagnose the problem. This was in the fall of 1983 when new cars were trying to combine computer controls with carburetors. It wasn't a totally successful combination. Only when fuel injection replaced carburetors did computer engine management become really practical. The test drive revealed that the surging and erratic running of the engine were due to a faulty program in the computer that would be annoying but not a problem which would strand her or cause an unsafe driving condition. I told her this and said it would be safe to drive to Topeka where her selling dealer would fix the problem under warranty. She was satisfied and my boss was happy I didn't take the vehicle into the shop for repair. This was one of many contacts with people that day and it would have been forgotten except for what happened several months later.

In April 1984, I was hired to be a staff chaplain at St. Francis Hospital and Medical Center in Topeka. I was absolutely thrilled. Finally, after years of training, I had the opportunity to practice my new profession. The owner of the dealership told me he was glad for me because he knew my heart wasn't in vehicle repair but in the arena of pastoral care. So I nervously showed up at St. Francis for my first day of work on April 14, 1984. I met my new boss (a Catholic Sister,) was oriented to the office, and shown around some of the nursing units. Everything was new to me and it was more than I could absorb in that first day. Sister then took me to the office of the CEO of the hospital, another Sister of Charity of Leavenworth Sister. As I entered the office, this President and CEO of the hospital looked at me, recognition showing on her face as she said these words: "I remember you. You were that young man who was so very kind to me when I was worried about my car. I know if you take as good care of our patients as you did me, you will be just fine."

Well, you guessed it. This CEO Sister was the same lady who came to our dealership that day. I wasn't supposed to take care of her. I was supposed to tell her to just drive on to Topeka without checking on her car at all. But, what if I had done that? Now, she would have looked at me, recognized me and said something very different. So in my mind I silently said, "Thank you, Jesus." Sometimes it matters to be who we really are and not to be what others think or believe we should be—or how others think we should act. Being real can be the best choice. In any case, God knew what to do and God arranged that "all things work together for good to them that love God" (Romans 8:28, KJV).

Of course, the verse also adds, "To them who are the called according to his purpose." Being real doesn't work unless being real is in accordance with God's will. It is a thing to remember. That day, it felt good to be real in accordance with God's will even though I had no idea what that will was at the time. God's will was for me to be hired at St Francis, which allowed me to be a chaplain for the next twenty-two years during which God had much to teach me. And, in the process of my learning, others were helped along on their journey as well. Truly, when God does the organizing it is a complete "win/win" situation. For sure, "Thank you, Jesus."

The "Knots Prayer"

Dear God:
Please untie the knots that are in my mind,
    my heart and my life.
Remove the have nots, the can nots and the do nots
    that I have in my spirit.

Erase the will nots, may nots, might nots
that may find a home in my heart.

Release me from the could nots, would nots
    and should nots that obstruct my life.

Help me to fear not, want not, worry not
and to let go of my afraid nots that prevent me from living fully.

And most of all, Dear God,
    I ask that You remove from my mind,
    my heart and my life
    all of the am nots that I have allowed to hold me back,
    especially the worry not thoughts
    that I am not good enough.

Amen.

Anonymous

"I Can't Trust You Anymore"

I had been working as chaplain on an inpatient alcohol and drug rehabilitation unit at St. Francis hospital for several years. During that time, hundreds of clients and their loved ones found relief from the power of addiction and resumed productive and happy lives. I was part of the clinical team who provided help in their successful recovery. From time to time, some would call me on the phone in order to ask for support in a particular life situation where they wanted input or guidance. Such contacts became routine as the years passed. There was a deep connection of trust and spiritual relationship that was very precious to me when these contacts happened. It made me realize that the effort put into recovery programs was truly worthwhile.

It happened that one of my previous patients called on the phone and I did attempt to call them back, only to find that they weren't home. I left a message on their voice mail. Soon after that I tried to contact them again, with the same results. Over the next several days, I made repeated attempts to get in touch with them but it never happened. I quit trying. Several months passed before I met the young man when he was in the hospital for some reason. He told me of a very difficult time he and his wife had gone through, and I asked him why he hadn't contacted me. He said, "I tried, but when you quit trying to call me back I realized that I couldn't trust you, so I found help somewhere else." Well, now, that hurt my pride and I remember being very defensive, making excuses and blaming faulty voice mail or something else for my failure to get back with him. After all, I tried several times. But the memory of the pain in his face as he told me, "I can't trust you anymore" still haunts me. No, I don't believe I really did anything wrong ethically. I did try to contact him, and he didn't contact me again when he could have done so. Nonetheless, I didn't follow through as I might have done. I did let it go, and I did quit trying to contact him after a number of tries that failed. I didn't keep on keeping on. No fault, no blame, but no excuse either.

Building trust is a fragile process. How long do we keep trying in a situation like that described above? I remember the Apostle Peter asking Jesus if he should forgive someone seven times before quitting. Jesus' reply was shattering when he said, "seventy times seven." (Matthew 18:22, KJV) In other words, we never quit trying. Of course, there is a practical limit in most cases, but I like the Jesus model of going after the lost sheep until it is found and looking for the lost coin until it is located and waiting for the lost son to return home until he appears at the door (Luke 15.) I didn't do that. So now, this young man could no longer trust me. That still hurts.

No, I'm not so co-dependent that I feel the need to save everyone or help everyone every time they ask. But, this was someone who had walked with me through the valley of the shadow of death in recovery, family week, individual sessions, groups, and fifth step. We shared pain together and we built trust. I broke that trust by not following up as he needed. He was the patient and I was the chaplain. He had a right to expect more of me than I gave and, as a consequence, the trust was broken. We haven't had contact since that time he told me he could no longer trust me. It has been many years. It feels as if it happened today.

I would rather remember and retell the successes that came from my ministry through the years. In this book, you'll find examples of how good things happened as a result of time spent with others in crisis. I feel good about those times of ministry, and I don't feel like a failure at all. But, it is still true that not every encounter was a success. I was blessed to have a supervisor in Atlanta who was a well-respected chaplain, professor, and therapist. He told us one day that, "On a good day, I am right eighty percent of the time." I was shocked. I thought the goal was to be right one hundred percent of the time when it came to counseling or spiritual help. Here he was admitting he was wrong at least one time out of each five. I've remembered that and so, I don't chastise myself too harshly when I make mistakes. However, I don't want to make excuses either. I did not need to have any insight or special wisdom to provide what my friend needed that day. All I needed to do was follow up and make the contact. I didn't do that.

It is important to be trustworthy and dependable. Making excuses is just another form of blame turned inside out. I cannot afford it. None of us can afford it. It is okay to make mistakes because we all do that. It is not okay to make excuses or to blame as a way to avoid being responsible. My friend paid the price of helping me learn a valuable lesson. He probably did find support elsewhere. I was the one who lost out, even more than he. It is a lesson I hope never to forget.

Lonely People

Look at all the people go.

So many different faces
Some seem happy, others not
All hustle and bustle to and fro
Attire varies from sharp to poor
Yet dress doesn't mean they're happy
Old ones, young and in between
Each on a search for what they need
Sometimes eyes meet and a smile comes
Other times it's pushing grumpily through
With a barely mumbled "sorry" or "excuse me"

Look at all the people distant in their own world

Not seeing, not hearing…alone in the crowd
They don't even realize they are so lonely
Their faces show stress and lines of worry
As they hasten to get done and go elsewhere
No time to experience the life all around
Or enjoy moments of pleasure at some sight
It's fun to call the clerks by name
They look up and respond with a few words
It's good to be noticed amidst the throng
Acknowledged for being a real person

Carol A Bond

"So, What Is The Exact Nature of My Wrongs?"

I had been working in addiction recovery for about four years when I met with this specific patient who was ready for her fifth step session with the chaplain. For those who are unfamiliar with what a fifth step is, take a look at the Twelve Steps of AA and you'll find that during fifth step, the client is expected to sit down with another person and confess their wrongs, exactly and specifically. I had been trained in this process, and I facilitated many sessions in the past, working toward some kind of resolution and of forgiveness on the part of the one doing fifth step. I felt good about the way I treated my clients, and the counselors reported that their patients responded well to having that experience with me. I was, in short, doing good work with very sensitive people in a very sensitive session. I was trusted by patients and by staff.

My patient on this particular day was a young lady in her mid-twenties who took her fifth step seriously and revealed and talked about events in her life that were very painful to admit. I was impressed. After she was finished revealing her "secret past," we talked about forgiveness until she understood and accepted that input very well. I thought we were done because we had completed the session just like I had been taught to do it. But she looked at me and said, "So, Cliff, what *is* the exact nature of my wrongs?"

I remember well how I just looked at her, blankly, for a few seconds with my mind going in high gear. Yes, she was right. The wording of fifth step did not say, "admitted our **wrongs.**" The fifth step said, "admitted the exact *nature* of our wrongs." Hmmmmm—there is a difference here. What she was asking for made perfect sense. What I did say to her was, "I have no idea—but we will find out." So, for the next half hour or so we did figure it out. Since that day, my goal in a fifth step is not to hear a person's confession of wrongs. That is a necessary part of the process, but the goal is to find the exact nature of those behaviors that were so heavily connected to regret, guilt, and shame. The difference is of profound importance.

If there is a common theme, a common thread, that ties all the wrongs together or a common denominator that fits every wrong committed, then it would be of great value to identify it. If identified, that exact nature of wrongs can shed great light on what we need to avoid in the future and what to work on in our recovery. It turns a very complex history composed of many individual incidents into "one thing" that can be more directly addressed. Admittedly, it is much easier to just hear a person recite his or her wrongs. But the value of doing a fifth step would be crippled if we settled for less than the Twelve Steps suggest.

I don't remember the name of my patient that day. I don't remember any of the specific wrongs she revealed. But, what she taught me revolutionized not only how I hear fifth steps but how I organize my sermons or structure a presentation for continuing education for professionals in health care. What is the one thing that we want to say? What is the core of our presentation? What is the sermon in a sentence? What is the pearl of great price that is worth more than all else in our world? All this and more came out of that question asked by a young lady who wanted more than anything else to find her sobriety.

In the years since, I've had many clients tell me their fifth step helped them a great deal. They walked out of my office with a better handle on their plans and they had a good idea of what had gotten them into trouble during the time of their addiction. Seldom is there an exact repeat in that nature of wrongs between clients. It is always somewhat different, and it takes some tough listening to find at times. But it is always there, even though I occasionally have to ask for the client's help in really identifying it properly. I may say, "It seems to me that the pattern I hear is…." and they might respond with, "I don't know—maybe." In that case, we look further. The goal is to find the exact nature of their wrongs, not to make me look wise and skilled. Often I don't know and so it takes a while to get there. However, if we are working together and if they are honest and if I am open and willing, it does happen—always. Like the Twelve Step Program is fond of saying, "It works if you work it."

What this means, concretely, is that it takes enormous honesty, risk, trust, and humility to do a fifth step. What professionals in the field of addiction treatment need to remember is that it takes the same for the counselor, sponsor, or chaplain as well. Otherwise all that is accomplished is an exchange of information.

Can you imagine how powerful it would be if all of us could find this "exact nature of our wrongs"? It is not only recovering addicts who would benefit because we could all find help in this process. But the situation will not be likely to happen because our society does not structure that into our experience. We are not likely to even admit the wrongs themselves, much less the nature of our wrongs. It is only when we know our life is in serious need of change that a person is willing to take that kind of step. But, again, can you imagine the benefit if we would all do this and go beyond confession to connection?

In this setting, on that important day, I admitted the exact nature of my wrongs as well. In my case, the exact nature was that I depended on my training and on "knowing" how to do my job. I wasn't open or willing to alter what I did or how I did it because I already knew how. When we know something for sure, we will not be likely to make changes. We get comfortable in a particular way of doing things because they worked in the past, and therefore they will work in the future. So, does that mean I've now settled into the familiar pattern also in looking for the exact nature of wrongs in every fifth step I hear? Perhaps there is always a need for caution here. The Twelve Step Program also says, "More will be revealed," which is a very powerful statement. But I don't believe the approach taught to me that day about fifth step is a problem because that very approach demands openness and willingness. In effect, I don't know what needs to happen with each client. I don't know how it needs to turn out. I am not in control. Instead, I am listening intently and allowing the moment to guide us where we need to be. It is this that makes me believe that it is the right approach, and why I trust the wisdom of the Twelve Steps themselves as they are applied and interpreted through the Holy Spirit to be a trustworthy guide. It is only when I begin to say, "I don't think there is any difference between admitting wrongs and admitting the exact nature of wrongs" that I begin to get into trouble. Yes, there is a difference. Am I willing to listen to that difference? Am I willing to listen to my patient, new to recovery, and learn from her or will I step back into my comfort zone and using my best professional voice say, "That is not really necessary—it is really the same thing?"

My journey on the road to real is not an easy one, as it turns out. My learning curve is filled with the need to make changes and choose different directions. I've had to listen to my patients and learn from them. I've needed to practice the same humility and trust I ask them to learn. I've had to identify the exact nature of my own wrongs and to work on the "one thing" that I need to do each day. Interestingly and with great excitement, I find that this changes all the time. Thank God for my friend who asked me her question. Her challenge has changed my life.

Healing Memories

Memory… is the mental faculty used to recall things
It's the recollection or remembrance of stored "stuff"
And it depends on the ability of the brain to bring to the forefront
Our personal collections of thought, experiences and the past

Memory is interesting for by the very process it is flawed
Our mind stores occurrences snug in little brain folders
And when we pull them out it is just our own paraphrase
Not necessarily the facts or reality but our own interpretation

Yet even then memory is influenced by how traumatic or delightful
Each happening was…and how we were feeling at the time
Illness, disease, mental abilities also determine clarity of the recall
Plus the situation or repercussions surrounding the remembrance

Then there are short term memories and long term memories…
Which all of us have unless some condition robs us of it
How each of our occurrences is stored whether flagged or hidden
Is determined by its impression or significance to us personally

So with all the many inconsistencies how can we trust ourselves
To remember correctly?…the answer is…we can't
All we are capable of is to recall as honestly as we are able
For it is our memory of how the incidence affected us

No one else will experience any event just like we did or do
There are too many variables in life and in the abilities of our senses
We can then enjoy our memories for they are ours alone
Shared possibly in part by others making them special

Thinking of the past conjures up many emotions and visions
They are part of what makes us what we are today
May our memories bring us comfort and acceptance
And may we forgive ourselves and others for shortcomings

Carol A Bond

"Oops—Wrong Room!"

When I worked at St. Francis hospital, there was a time when I would post on my office door a daily "Far Side" cartoon. I would often hear footsteps stop outside even when the door was closed, and then a chuckle, followed by retreating footsteps. I had a number of employees who made it a regular part of their day and who were disappointed when I was gone on vacation and the daily cartoons weren't posted. One in particular was a favorite of mine, which showed an Alien Being opening a classroom door at a university and after seeing the shocked look on the faces of the very humanoid people in the class saying, "Oops—wrong room!" That cartoon cracks me up.

Back in the mid 1980's, I was asked to give a presentation to a group of about fifty Baptist preachers concerning chaplaincy and my ministry with patients in a hospital. I knew many of these men personally and had even worked with a few professionally. I was pleased to have the opportunity to share for approximately an hour about my specialized branch of ministry. I worked in a three hundred and fifty-bed acute care medical center with patients who experienced every kind of illness and problem. Part of my work was on our "Chemical Dependency Treatment Center," where I worked with those recovering from various addictions. In a previous chapter, I said that my interest in addiction treatment came from something a supervisor told me in Atlanta, Georgia, in 1981 at Grady Hospital during my first quarter of CPE. This supervisor said that he noticed that many of the verbatims I presented in my educational groups were about patients who were alcoholic. I responded that I was not aware of that. In true supervisor fashion, he said, "Cliff, I think you have an alcoholic personality!" Remember, we Baptist preachers do NOT have alcoholic personalities! I knew he was wrong.

Now, let us get back to my presentation several years later to a group of Baptist pastors. I was introduced and stood up at the podium looking out at the expectant faces of those present. Without really thinking, I said what I often said to a group which was, "Hi, my name is Cliff and I am an addict." I realized after seeing the startled and confused looks on the faces of those men that this was probably not what they had expected so I then said, "Oops, I forgot where I was for a minute." (Oops—wrong room) I then gave an explanation of my work as a chaplain, including work with recovering persons. I believe I did a good job and it was interesting to those pastors. What was not expected was that after the initial "Nice job, Cliff" responses, several pastors came up, one at a time, and quietly admitted that they had a problem with alcohol or drugs and had never told anyone. And nobody in their church really knew about it. Actually, five of the fifty came up and admitted they had a secret addiction and wanted to know what they needed to do.

Amazingly, I wasn't in the wrong room after all. I learned that day that ten percent of the pastors who were leaders of their congregations had addictions that were a problem, and they didn't know where to go for help. My guess is that there were another five who had a problem but didn't come and talk with me about it. These were men who were counselors and pastors to people who lived in a society where there are many who have alcohol or drug addictions but keep that a secret. I had no idea. Then I made the connection to what my supervisor said to me years before, which was, "Cliff, I believe you have an alcoholic personality." Rather than argue just what that means, the point is that I wasn't aware of my own addiction any more than these pastors were. Denial is truly the name of addiction, especially when it strikes "good" people.

So, I wasn't in the wrong room and the pastors who came to hear about hospital chaplaincy weren't in the wrong room either. In Twelve Step Recovery terms, what I said that day was "A God Thing" and not a mistake. And, even more to the point, those pastors and many others see addiction or alcoholism as being equivalent to a skid row bum or someone lying in a gutter without a job and without hope or purpose. Here I was, a respected chaplain in a large hospital saying that I was an addict. And that invited a response from other "nice" and respected men to say that they had a problem also. One of my good friends who had been known to me for many years before my chaplaincy training talked to me one day about that. He asked why I was working "with those kind of people," meaning alcoholics. I responded that I liked working with them and then added, "And, I AM one of 'those kind' of people."

His response was classic when he said, "But Cliff, you are not a real addict!" When I asked him what a real addict looked like, he couldn't tell me. But when I said, "Do you mean someone lying in the gutter with a needle in their arm, all filthy and smelly?" he said that was what he meant. I told him that was only about three percent of all the addicts we are likely to encounter. Many addicts looked just like me.

In "Far Side" terms, we all say, "Oops, wrong room" when we feel out of place. We don't want to feel like an alien. We don't want to be different. So, when we have problems we explain them away or even go into denial where we cannot see it even in ourselves.

Actually, we are all in the same room. We all have some kind of problem. It is only when we finally accept the way things are that we can be courageous enough to change. I am so grateful to that supervisor who was direct enough to say to me what needed to be said. I am grateful to the many recovering addicts and alcoholics who have trusted me with their stories. I am grateful that I can admit that I am a recovering addict because it is much better than being a non-recovering addict.

In truth, I seldom use the terms "addict" or "alcoholic" when I meet with clients. When they say they don't believe they are, I say that I don't know either. What I ask then is if there are problems in their life that are worse when they drink or use drugs. And even though the problems are there, do they still drink or use drugs anyway. That is the issue. Labels are stigmas. Behavior is what we really need to look at—and consequences. When we do that, we find that truly, we are all in the same room. We all need to work on some defect in our lives that hurts us or those we love AND WHICH WE KEEP ON DOING ANYWAY! "Oops—wrong room" is a cartoon. Life is not.

If you never…

If you never do what you've never done
      If you never become what you've wanted to be
If you never see what you wanted to see
      If you never realize what you've dreamed about
If you never find what you've searched for
      If you never receive what you've desired
If you never travel what roads you've wanted
      If you never give what you have to give
If you never pray what you've worried about
      If you never feel what you've seen others suffer

If you never share what you've felt inside
      If you never believe what you've been taught
If you never trust what love you've been given
      If you never seek what you've never experienced
If you never fail what you've tried to do
      If you never cry what pain you've carried
If you never shout what joy you've had
      If you never remember what you've been given
If you never be what you've prayed to be…

Then do it, be it, see it, experience it now
For you haven't fully lived
until you've stretched your
mind,
body,
spirit,
faith,
hope
and dreams

DO IT NOW!!!!!!!!!!!!!!!!!!

Carol A Bond

"Who Are *YOU*?!"

There are some things a chaplain isn't accustomed to hearing as he or she makes rounds in the hospital. But let me explain what happened one morning after team report on the oncology floor at St. Francis hospital. The Spiritual Care Department at this hospital was supervised by a Roman Catholic Sister of the order that owned and operated this fine institution of medical care. I had worked there for a number of years along with other chaplains, providing pastoral support to patients and staff. She trusted me to provide appropriate and spiritual support in a caring and compassionate manner. We were expected not to curse, nor were we accustomed to hearing patients use rough talk with us except, for instance, when an emergency room patient was in pain, or drunk, or very afraid. But this was the exception, not the rule.

On this morning, I entered the room of a male patient about my age, at that time about fifty-five. He was a strong, young man in his prime, looking very fit and capable. However, he had just been diagnosed with cancer and he was waiting for tests that would determine any needed treatment. He was in bed; I was on my feet. He was a captive in a strange environment, and I was free to walk about as I pleased. I was not sick and he had cancer.

I was friendly enough when I entered the room but he looked up from his bed, saw my name tag, realized I was a chaplain/minister/religious person and said in a loud, intimidating voice, "Who are

You?!" (And his exact words included some rough words not used in polite company.) Maybe he expected to scare me off, perhaps he just wanted to shock the minister, or maybe he just didn't know what to say and said what he did because that was just how he was. At any rate, I didn't think or meditate or even hesitate. I just responded and without any real pause, said, repeating some of his words and echoing his mood, "I'm the chaplain, that's who I am—***who are you***?!"

Now, I have never, ever before used that approach with a patient at any hospital. Actually, I never said it again. But, much like the quote from Steve McQueen in the movie *The Magnificent Seven,* "it seemed like a good idea at the time." In response, he looked at me for a second and then said, "Sit down," motioning me to the chair by his bed. We talked and he told me about his diagnosis, his work, his family, and eventually, about his anxiety and fear. I saw him many times after that and was introduced to his wife when she came in. We stayed in touch for a couple of years after that from time to time, just to see how things were going. It turned out to be a very profitable relationship for everyone concerned. So, what does this say about confessions on the journey to being real?

I believe that this particular man, in that particular circumstance, with that particular chaplain, made a connection that would not have been made in any other way at that particular time. What is there about being real that is so difficult? It has a lot to do with the willingness to take a risk. We have so many layers of convention and social rules that it is profoundly complicated when we introduce ourselves to others. There is no one "right" way. There are guidelines and that day, some of those guidelines were broken or at the very least, bent severely.

All I do know, for certain, is that a connection was made that became very important in that man's care. My response came out of who I am; who I really am, and I still believe that being real is a better choice than being "right." So, I still believe that in that moment, it was the best thing to say to him. Why? That is a good question and it deserves more than a quick answer.

My patient was being real. He wasn't playing the "be nice to the nice pastor" game. He wasn't being polite. He wasn't hiding behind conventions and social niceties. In his fear and his feeling of powerlessness, he was real. And, to a significant extent, he was taking a risk with me. It would have been an insult to ignore all of that. He knew I wasn't making fun of him and he knew, I believe, that my response was tailored just for him and was not my usual manner of speaking. He dared to be real. He took that risk with me. Any other kind of response would have reduced the interchange to a less real event. We both took a risk and trust came out of it.

There is another answer to the question of why I responded as I did. I trust my instinct, my gut, and my intuition. I believe that is another way of saying I trust the Holy Spirit. I know there could be some who would disagree with that, in this instance, but I do believe it. There is a place for plain speech. As my supervisor in Atlanta said to me, "Sometimes the nicest thing to do for someone is the not nice thing." Being nice is what we are taught to do. Being real is sometimes preferable. I was raised and reared in a devout Seventh Day Baptist family. There was never, ever any cursing, using the Lord's name in vain or such. That, I believe is a good thing. As a minister of the Gospel I have become a student of the Bible and have been surprised from time to time, however, at the direct speech used by Jesus during his ministry. In Matthew 25:41, for example, Jesus actually goes so far as to say he will one day tell people to "go into the eternal fire prepared for the devil...." (NIV) I find that very interesting and impossible to just ignore because I take everything Jesus said very seriously.

Sometimes, direct and even rough words fit a situation best. I spoke from my heart to a man who was speaking from his. We used words that need to be reserved for very unusual circumstances, not used casually for no purpose and certainly never, ever, uttered in vain. Actually, I believe that the words uttered that day became a blessing. How can that be? It is so because we were being honest and taking a risk with each other. Being real often needs that element of risk. I spoke out of who I am not just what I do. So, who am I? I am the chaplain; that is who I am. When you are in distress, you can say anything you want to me, and I will respond as honestly and directly as I can. My patients all knew that. I hope they always will.

Motives

When I say you ought to do this or that…
Am I really saying I want you to do it
Yet am not able to be that brazenly honest?

When I say you should do this or that…
Am I saying there is some standard or reason
That dictates you do it…and thus absolves me?

When I criticize something you have done or redo it…
Am I really parroting what someone said to me…or
Am I so fearful or so arrogant that my way is the only way?

When I am adamant when you are taking things to work…
Am I really so afraid of someone taking advantage of you…
Or am I really selfish and feel we'll lose those things?

When I deal with myself, my motives and my expectations
While I may mean well and have the best of intentions,
Oft times it is me, my stuff and my beliefs that are really the issue.

Carol A Bond

"Our Parents Are Not Perfect"

In the fall of 1989, my wife and I renewed our vows in a twenty-fifth wedding anniversary celebration at our home church in Nortonville, Kansas. This is where we grew up, where we were baptized and where we were married. Our children were baptized there, and my ordination as a minister was held there in 1982. Many friends and relatives attended who were very pleased to honor us as a couple who work in ministry for our Lord. We sat up front, facing the congregation as our grown children each stood up and said a few words about their parents. The first to speak was our daughter, who seemed to be more than a little nervous, but her voice was clear as she began to speak. The first words out of her mouth were, "Our parents are not perfect." I could hear an audible intake of air from the congregation—a sort of gasp—as those words sunk in. She then continued and said, "But what we love about our parents is that they are not the same as they were ten years ago. They have grown and changed right along with us." She said other things as well, but those words were echoed by our sons as they spoke to the gathered group as well. They are precious words. After the service, we had a reception in the church basement but nobody talked about what our children said. I have pondered that many times since then, and I have come to believe that many would be afraid to have their children be that honest about them. I am pleased at both aspects of our children's statements. No, we are not perfect. Yes, we have changed and grown. In all honesty, I would much rather be imperfect and able to change or grow than to be "perfect" and be the same person after years of life.

There was a time in our lives when our family was in therapy for some issues going on. In one session, our daughter, who was then nineteen years old, spoke to me and said, "I don't want a chaplain, I don't want a pastor. I don't want a therapist, I don't want a counselor. I want a father. Please let me make my own mistakes because sometimes my mistakes are all that are really mine." That was painful to hear but it needed to be said.

Our children were what are sometimes referred to as "P.K's." (Pastor's Kids) From early childhood they understood the need to be quiet in church, to attend meetings and gatherings that were sometimes boring, and to meet people that many children did not become acquainted with. They went with us to the Rescue Mission in Kansas City where I would preach to the so called "skid row bums" who were homeless and hungry. We ate the same hot dog soup served to those men, and our children never complained. We went to the inner city areas where children played in the street and our kids, not yet of school age, asked why they didn't play in their yards. They were thoughtful when we told them these children didn't have a fenced yard with a swing set and a big dog to keep them safe. Our three kids grew up with enough but never as much as many of their playmates had. Yet they understood others didn't have nearly what they enjoyed. They never did take what they had for granted. Our children grew up with that kind of sensitivity. So what did they mean when they said we weren't perfect? What did our daughter mean when she asked me to be a father, not a pastor to her? It took me at least a year to figure that out.

Several years before, as was our custom, our family gathered for breakfast before we each went our separate ways, either to work or to school. Two of our children were old enough at that time to drive, so all three drove themselves the several miles to school at Oskaloosa from where we lived in the country. Carol worked as a traveling nurse reviewing nursing homes for the State of Kansas. I was working as a service writer in a car dealership in Lawrence. I sat down that morning and noticed some flowers in a vase. I asked what the flowers were for. The children looked up and said, "They are for Clay's birthday." Clay was their brother who died at birth seventeen years before and whom they had, of course, never seen. That year we had three children in high school: a senior, a sophomore, and a freshman. Clay would have filled it out perfectly by being a junior. Every day was a reminder of someone being absent. We were not complete. They remembered. That is the sort of children we had and they were the ones who dared to say to a church full of people that their parents weren't perfect. And that is why we listened to what they said and appreciated the second part, which stated that we had grown—that we had changed. And they liked the change. Now, my daughter was asking me to change again. And I was willing.

After graduating from high school, Camille went to college for a year before moving to Wichita, Kansas. She was now on her own but I was still in my parent mode of feeling responsible to guide or govern some of her choices. She would gently say to me, when I did that, "Dad, you are doing it again." I would pause and say, "I am?" She would respond and say, "Yes, you are, but that's okay." We would then renegotiate our conversation to where I would make some observations or perhaps even some suggestions, but I would stop short of telling her what she needed to do. That went on for a year after what she said to me in the therapy session. I practiced the art of "letting go without letting go," which any parent knows is a very difficult task indeed.

One day Camille and I drove to Kansas City to shop for a truck for Carol. We had a wonderful time with her driving my little hot rod car I had built. We looked at trucks, we ate lunch together, and on the ride back to Oskaloosa, she began to talk of times in her childhood when she felt as if she'd been adopted, when she started to run away from home and other memories that I had not been aware of. I was amazed. I said, "You never told me any of this." She said, "No." I then said, "You couldn't, could you?" She said, "No." I said, "I wouldn't have listened, would I?" She said, "No—but that's okay because you are listening now."

It's important to let our children make their own mistakes—as scary as that sounds. My relationship with my children changed and, I believe, improved because of what they told me through the years. I learned from them just as they learned from me. And that is very profound. We have learned to negotiate and not to operate by edict. "Because I said so" is no longer an adequate response. Perhaps it never was. They have indeed grown up as "P.K.'s" but they are so much more than that. They have learned to remember the birthday of a brother they never knew. They dared to challenge a parent to grow and change. They asked for the right to make their own decisions on some choices even before they were out of high school. We as a family learned to share and to avoid control as the primary way of relating.

So, now we know that we as parents are not perfect. That is really quite humorous because the same could be said about any and all parents. What cannot be said, sadly, is that sometimes we don't change and grow and become different in a healthy way. God allows us as His children to make mistakes. He could prevent those choices but instead gives guidelines that we can disobey and often do, to our peril. But, if God allows us to make our mistakes and learn from them, isn't that a pattern for our human parenting also? As we journey on our own road to real, it is a thing to consider. For Carol and I, we are happy to be imperfect and also happy to have grown, changed, and become better as a result.

Life's Candle

The simple wick is lit with the flame of the match
And the candle springs to life sending rays of light
Flickering and reaching to the dark areas of the room.

Though small in size the flame reaches high and wide
Comforting through its radiance and illumination.
The patterns flow and ebb, ever changing and bright.

The dance is slow at times, or fast as air currents change.
It stimulates the visual awareness and draws the eye
To its core of light even beyond imagination.

Its brilliance cheery, warm and so vital
The intense gleam continues as long as fuel and air exist
And when the source wanes the flame gradually ceases.

So like the candle are we as we walk through life
When our quiet heart is ignited by the Spirit with its fire
A life of passionate caring and service flares into being.

We flicker and move and reach those areas of need.
Though we may not be huge in stature we can reach far
And comfort and ease those that are searching in the dark.

Our form and design change with the current of the day
Moving slowly or dancing brightly as the energy flows
Our center being glows, exuding warmth and acceptance.

It is hope and faith, vital and alive beyond expectations
Then when our time is done the intensity, ardor and energy ebb
Our wick's flame goes out and we rest in the Light of the Spirit.

Carol A Bond

Faith, Family, Friends

Wisdom comes from those who "have been there and done that," meaning only those who have had experience have the right to an opinion about things that are important. I worked with alcoholics and drug addicts for nine years before changing my focus to general hospital work. My primary assignment now was to be with our cancer patients. Our hospital provided three cancer care areas: a medical floor, a special unit where chemotherapy was administered, and a radiation oncology department where external beam radiation and radiation implants were used. I was assigned to all areas and found I needed to learn some new chaplaincy skills for this new clientele. Of course, some of what I already knew could be applied to cancer patients and their families, but there were significant differences as well. Once again, I determined to learn from the experts: the patients themselves and the families and friends who supported them.

For one thing, cancer treatment is a high-tech, very scientific process, unlike substance abuse treatment, which uses psychotherapy, group interaction, behavioral change, and some medications as primary treatment methods. Addiction recovery doesn't require multi-million dollar machines and very expensive and dangerous chemicals and isotopes in order to be effective. In addiction therapy, surgery wasn't expected and physical pain wasn't a usual symptom. But again, I wasn't trying to understand all this on my own—I had guidance from the physicians, nurses, radiation techs, and others who provided input. However, the primary source of my education came from the patients themselves. For the most part, they were very willing to share once they found that someone really wanted to listen. As in addiction recovery, cancer was no respecter of persons; all ages, ethnic groups, genders, and every category included in humanity can be a cancer patient. Cancer is truly an equal opportunity disease. But, so was addiction; that reality was not difficult to learn. There may be high-risk situations, but there was no clear cut "cause" for cancer any more than there had been for addiction.

Soon I was being invited by the staff to visit with the patients and their families. The physicians allowed me to use their individual examination rooms, flagging my presence with a patient just as they did when a nurse or a doctor visited them. Slowly, a trust relationship began to develop with the staff and with the patients. I was part of the team. I didn't use any kind of standardized questionnaire nor did I do any official assessment. I was asked to see patients who were experiencing significant grief, fear, anger, or were having questions about "why me?" that the staff felt the chaplain could be helpful in treating. Most of the patients were receptive and even grateful to find their emotional or spiritual pain was being addressed just as intentionally as their physical difficulty.

Often, after a trust relationship was established, I'd ask them what it was that helped them cope in the difficult times in addition to the quality medical care received. I was amazed to find their answers were similar and also profoundly simple. Almost always, their answer was that what they needed most of all was their faith, their family, and their friends. Often, those exact words were used although sometimes they would say it was their church, or important people in their life, or their husband, children, etc. But the important reality that came through time after time was faith, family, and friends gave them hope.

Some of my patients had money, power, prestige, fame, youth, or other circumstances that are valued in our society. They never said any of these were important in the difficult days of cancer treatment. It never, ever happened.

Eventually, I used those three categories as assessment tools for a person's spiritual condition whether they were cancer patients, addicts, or patients in pre-op. I wanted to know if they had faith, family, and friends in their arsenal of weapons against their condition. If those three were present, then I felt their medical situation was being supported spiritually regardless of how _religious_ their faith might be, how _many_ family they had or _how_ their friends might dress or talk. I began to look at my own life and came to realize how very wealthy I was because I had all three available to me. I began to appreciate the "attitude of gratitude" that is talked about in addiction recovery. I began to appreciate how this had enormous power in the fight against cancer as well.

The effects of chemotherapy or radiation can be documented and tracked or graphed providing percentages and predicted outcomes. My work as a chaplain didn't have those kinds of markers, so we would talk about "the X factors." When patients asked what the percentage of survival was, I told them I didn't know—talk with their doctor—but I did know that attitude, prayer, faith, support, hope, and such had a powerful effect on outcomes even though we didn't know exactly how or why. In other words, the evidence showed that faith, family, and friends could affect their physical recovery from cancer. And that allowed me to become part of their faith and their friends. In some cases it was almost as though I was "family."

The journey toward being real has been, and continues to be, one filled with its rewards. It is certain the journey cannot be completed alone because being real involves relationship with another, always. Even the mystics who retreated to isolated places for meditation had that relationship with the God of their understanding for company. I wouldn't trade what my cancer patients taught me for all the fortune, fame, or power in the world. They taught me that faith, family, and friends are the foundation for all we need. They also taught me that faith, family, and friends are essential; without them, we are stripped of the resources we need if we are to do battle against any disease.

They taught me that faith, family, and friends are essential companions on our road to real.

Cancer

Cancer...the word that stops a person's world
The death knell sounds in their ears...
Knees tremble, hands shake, hearts shudder
Emotions run amuck and fear runs rampant
To have an adult loved one stricken is terrible

    And even more traumatic when it's a child
    The physician goes over the possibilities
    The treatments seem overwhelming and scary
    The waiting game for chemo and radiation
    Is as scary as moving forward to the inevitable

So many tests, tubes, medicines and jargons
A new language has to be learned just to cope
Chemo begins and they feel so sick
Hair is lost...blood counts go down
Further therapy has to be put on hold

    Until the counts go back up enough
    Fear strikes...will it be too late to help?
    The past and the future meet amidst reality
    What was... is no longer and may never be again
    Accepting what is strikes terror to the very soul

Adapting to the changes is so terribly difficult
But to survive, much adjusting must be done
Most stand on faith...shakily believing in God
Despite the disease and all appearances...
Each day is met on bended knee and hope

    While clinging to the Word keeps sanity in the storm
    All prepare for the worst while hoping for the best
    Hanging on to faith and faithful supporters
    They talk with others in the strange world of cancer
    Reveling in the good days between treatments...

Keeping vigil at the bedside on bad days...
Struggling to keep sanity and hold depression at bay
While dealing with the anger, sadness, grief
Injustice, and the longing for the past time of health
They wonder how to get through each long day

    Without falling completely to pieces in a heap...
    Or crying incessantly giving in to the sorrow...
    Questioning if it will ever be all right again...
    While trying to maintain a hopeful demeanor...
    So the loved one won't know their horrid turmoil

Touching the face of their loved one
Speaking quietly
Uttering prayers and words of love and encouragement
Holding their hand and being there through every stage
They continue on with the hope for new times after cancer

Carol A Bond

"Whatever It Is You Do…"

One of the great benefits of working in a medical center as a chaplain is that we are part of the care team and as such are accepted as part of the healing process. We go to team meetings; we visit with physicians, therapists, nurses, and other professionals and are requested at times to intervene in particular situations. On our oncology floor, our team met daily to discuss the care plan for each of our patients. Present were the charge nurse or the patient's primary care nurse, social worker, clinical nurse specialist, dietician, chaplain, and sometimes other healthcare professionals. We would decide whose services were needed at that particular time so we wouldn't duplicate interventions or ignore needs. There is often overlap between social work and chaplaincy, but we worked through that by mutual agreement each morning. We didn't compete but complemented each other to the benefit of the patients, families, and staff.

Physicians weren't often in that meeting but were quite often right outside the room, charting and reviewing plans for each of their patients. One morning I was charting on one of the patients and a physician came by to sit beside me as he reviewed the progress of his patient. As he read the notes, he pondered for a few moments before discussing the situation about that patient, part of which I understood and part of which was medical information that escaped me. However, eventually he looked at me and said, "Cliff, whatever it is that you do, go back and do it with_____." (this patient)

That statement was very interesting. We had worked together for several years. We had cared for the same patients, and he had read my charting on numerous occasions. An attitude of trust developed so he believed there was an aspect of care I could provide that was different from what other team members gave. Although he didn't know exactly what it was I did in the room, he was confident it was beneficial. And so, he asked for my assistance.

I know my limitations and am comfortable having them. I don't try to diagnose or prescribe. I am happy to refer to others whose expertise is needed. "What did the doctor say?" was an everyday question asked many times by me when I visited with patients. I knew who was in charge, and I appreciated and respected that burden of responsibility. My input was limited to my area of skill and knowledge, which was fine with me and trusted by the other team members. I didn't try to be the nurse, or the physical therapist, or the dietician. I was happy to work with a social worker whose knowledge of community resources was much more complete than mine. That didn't mean nurses never prayed for patients or social workers didn't recommend a pastor or a church. But, like the physician that day, they recognized some information is trusted more when it comes from a person identified in a particular role. If I say to a patient that they are forgiven, it has more credibility for most people than if a physical therapist, nurse, or physician says it. The physician, that day, wanted the patient to find realistic hope and spiritual strength in the face of very intimidating circumstances. That physician believed I was the one who could provide that interchange. And the physician was willing to admit that, although he could go in and perhaps say much the same thing; it wouldn't be the same—because of the roles.

There were times when we chaplains would take blessed oil onto the nursing units and ask if any of the nurses or physicians wanted to have their hands blessed and a prayer offered for their ministry of healing. Usually the response was positive. At other times, I would greet a physician in the hallway and ask how he or she was doing that day. "You take such good care of so many people, how are you?" I'd ask, and sometimes the physician leaned against the wall and visited for a few minutes, grateful to have someone ask them how they were. At other times, I dropped by and visited one of the executives of the medical center and asked them how they were doing, or what was going on in their life. I found these professionals were often hungry for contact that wasn't just medical or technical. "Whatever it is that you do" became a blueprint for what I did in the course of the day. I was the chaplain. It was a thing to remember and was taught again to me by the physician that day at the nursing station.

But, in addition, the physician acknowledged that he didn't know what it was, exactly, that I did for the patient beyond a general understanding. What impressed me was that there was reality, honesty, and humility shown by the physician all for the benefit of the patient. There was trust in the relationship we had built through time. It wasn't the physician's intention, I am sure, but his words reinforced my belief that spiritual care is unique, important, and too often overlooked in far too many hospitals. Physicians frequently aren't trained in spiritual care at all but do appreciate the support it gives their patients. Each of us has something that we do. So, "whatever it is that you do, go and do it with that person," whoever that person might be in your life. Claim your calling and your own particular gifts.

"Try Not—DO—or do not."

(Yoda, in Star Wars)

Risk taking and decision making
Are all part of our growth process in order to be.

If we don't take the risks of changing behavior
Learning, trying something new, challenging ourselves
We cannot see who we really are and want to be.

If we analyze everything we do, say or try
It's a malevolent prejudging of who or what we are
And may thwart our desires and our future hopes.

Questioning all our decisions and rating them
As good, bad or indifferent stymies our progress
Blocks our spontaneity and causes fear and worry.

Decisions are just that...making a choice...
Making a choice is selecting and accepting
The consequences and responsibility for that choice.

Sometimes we don't know what we want to do...
We hem-haw around and do nothing chancy
To find out we must start in some direction.

There can be no discovery if we don't search.

There can be no vistas if we don't begin a journey.

As Yoda says: "try not...do"...
If we want to complete a dream and don't do so
It would seem that is not our inner desire.

It was talk, wishful thinking or our ability is lacking
Listening to our self...our intuition...our awareness
Hearing the rhythm of our soul and desires.

Taking time for quiet, tunes us into the still small voice
And guides us into wholeness, faith and purpose
With freedom to take risks and make decisions.

No guilt...no shame...no blame...no excuse.

Carol A Bond

"Should" Is the Word of Death

I began working with clients who were addicted to alcohol, drugs, gambling, or other compulsive behaviors in the early 1980's. At that time, crack cocaine was a major player in the addiction community before meth became prominent. Quite a few of my clients were successful professionals whose lives became out of control and who lost everything to the seduction of cocaine. I saw a bumper sticker on the back of a beat-up car one day that read, "My other car went up my nose!" Such was the situation for many young, upwardly mobile professionals in those days. One of the young men I became acquainted with was a lawyer whose addiction resulted in complete financial ruin and numerous other losses that went along with his sense of failure, stupidity, and shame. During his twenty-eight day inpatient treatment, we talked many times and he began to open up and share his fears and the guilt and shame that dominated his life. As he shared during the many times we met together, a pattern began to emerge that included his perceived inability to live up to the hopes and expectations of his family. My client realized that he had never felt good enough to satisfy others and his sense of failure was a major component of his addiction. I was impressed with his ability to come to that depth of insight in only a four-week treatment process. After completion of inpatient therapy, he chose to continue in the aftercare, or "continuing care," group that met once a week. His life was still in financial ruin, his law practice was destroyed, and he was working as a clerk in a Kwik Shop. There is nothing shameful about that employment, but it was a far cry from the six-figure income he once had as a lawyer. He was feeling very depressed and hopeless when he came to the weekly meetings, but he continued attending them and also regular NA meetings as well. He was working a good program, but at this point he was still feeling negative about himself. In effect, he was continuing the low self-worth that he had learned from his family growing up. He was doing to himself what others had done to him. No unusual surprise there.

I remember very well one particular continuing care meeting. About twenty recovering persons were present, sharing with each other what helped and what didn't help them in their efforts to live a life without addiction. My lawyer friend was sitting somewhat out of the circle of chairs, a bit by himself and not saying much or contributing to the general discussion. Suddenly he broke his silence and said, "Should is the word of death." He said it rather quietly but everyone heard, and we all quit talking. We looked at him and after a moment we asked him what he said. He repeated it and as he now looked up at us he said a bit more loudly and clearly, "SHOULD is the word of DEATH!"

Well now, that started a lively discussion for sure! What did he mean by that? So, he explained and we listened as his voice grew stronger and his understanding of what he said began to find words. He was, after all, a lawyer, so his speaking became very impassioned and convincing. We witnessed a remarkable metamorphosis. He was good at what he did, and he began to realize it. That realization began to make a lie out of what he had been told about himself by significant people in his life. He was good enough. He had not failed. But, he believed he failed because he had not lived up to what his father and others in his life told him he "should" do and "should" be. Up until that moment, he hadn't done what he chose to do; he merely tried to live up to the expectations of others. And, of course, that hadn't worked very well. We don't do well when our behaviors, even our good ones, are ruled primarily by the "shoulds."

Interestingly, when we begin to make good choices, many of the behaviors we choose will look identical to those we were told we "should" do—but they come from within, not from without. That difference, however, is far more important than some people might believe. I've thought of that night's continuing care group many times since. I've borrowed that concept and used it in many sessions and have become known as the counselor or the chaplain who doesn't use that word. My clients learn that I will never "should" on them.

My friend worked on his own recovery, eventually remarried (his addiction cost him his first marriage), and began a law practice in a small town near to his home area. He and his wife had a compassion for children whose lives had been ruled by a sense of failure and so they worked with many of those kids through the years. He sent pictures of himself and his family for several years after his successful treatment. I treasure them because they show a man who no longer fails to live up to the expectations of others but who sets his own expectations and lives up to them instead. He doesn't do what others say he "should" do. He now makes choices and sets goals that free him to be who he really is, and he can feel good about that. He actually feels good about himself. He is now free.

So, just what is it that he taught me as I journey on my own road to being real? Most of us are governed to a great extent by what we are told and taught we "should" do or be. We use the word "should" a lot. Doing what we "should" do is considered a mark of responsibility and of maturity. And in some ways that is true but perhaps we would do well to learn something more about that word. "Should is the word of death," my friend said. Just what did he mean by that? Many of my behaviors fit with what others believe I should do—but that isn't the reason I do them. I don't do good things because I should do them. I do them because they are good things to do. There is a major difference here. Dr. James Fowler has done extensive work on this topic, and he taught me much during my days at Emory. Being a "law-abiding citizen," for example, is thought to be a very high ethical standard and it often is. However, law-abiding citizens could, and did, turn Jewish people over to the police during WWII in Germany. There were some who disobeyed the law and weren't law-abiding citizens. We've made movies and written books about them. We see these persons as examples of superior ethical behavior, and we are right in doing so. I suppose we could argue and say their behavior was what they truly "should" have done, according to a higher law. Perhaps this is so. I would not disagree. But it still doesn't answer what my friend came to realize that night in continuing care.

He was reacting to the "should" from outside himself. I've come to the place where I do my best to use other words or phrases instead of the easily spoken "should" word. My father and I discussed this one day, and he finally asked me, "So why do you do what you do if it is not because you should do it?" As much as possible, I try to do what is right, loving, and good. I don't kiss my wife because I should. I don't visit my patients because I should. I don't help persons with addictions find a relationship with a Higher Power that can restore them to sanity because I should. I do what I do because it is what I choose to do. There is no "should" there at all. Doing good things only because we should do them is really lame. In that way, "should is the word of death."

Yes, this is a difficult concept to wrap our minds around. But, even so, I agree with my friend who discovered that his sense of failure, his anger, his resentment, his low self-worth, and so much more came from his need to live up to an external guide that left him feeling like a failure. When the desire to do the right thing became internalized, he found his place in life and was successful. Not only that, he could enjoy his success because it was his. He didn't develop a caring life because it was something he "should" do. He became what he became because it was his choice and something he desired more than anything else.

Use the word "should" if you must. Allow the "shoulds" from others to govern and direct your life if you choose. My friend taught me that should is far too dangerous a word to hear or speak lightly. So, I choose to "avoid the woid" whenever possible. It takes some thought and it takes intentional choice, but that's not a bad thing either. I really have come to believe that "should is the word of death." There is a better way and somewhere, in your heart, you suspect it is true also. "Should" is not a good companion if we are on the road to real. Those two words, "should" and "real," somehow don't fit together well. Enjoy the journey—should free.

Decisions

The terror of making decisions is not the decision itself…
But the "what if's" or the "maybe I should have's" that rattle us
Then when the decision is made those doubts still remain
And if all doesn't work out as it "should" have…
We lose confidence in our abilities to think clearly.

A wise person said…when a decision is made…it is the right one
At least for that time period with the knowledge at that time
It isn't healthy to second guess ourselves…we can only learn
There's no way to know the outcome of our choices
Until time passes--for hind sight comes only after the fact.

So many things influence our lives and general well being…
Our decisions, the experiences we have whether good or "bad"
How we see ourselves, our physical appearance, our health
Our mental, emotional and spiritual condition and our relationships
Each has a bearing on how we function and perceive our self and life.

Realizing those things that we can control and making changes appropriately
Accepting those things we cannot control and going forward afresh
Striving toward reasonable goals and praying for guidance to do God's will
Changing with age and limitations yet seeking ever new endeavors
Being our best come-what-may makes us revitalized and redirected caregivers.

May on this day we value the decisions made and the grace to accept them
May we appreciate who we are, where we've been and what we have to give
May we anticipate service in different avenues and continue to blossom
May we claim our hopes and dreams and work to make them happen
May we continue to aspire to give, to love, to inspire and to ease burdens.

Carol A Bond

"Go and Sin Some More"

Making mistakes is no fun and having someone else know how many mistakes we make is even worse. We want to appear in control. We like others to admire us; we want to feel good about ourselves at the end of the day. We would be very upset if other people "found out" about any of our secret behaviors. Quite simply, we don't dare to be honest, very often, about the inner struggles and the outward actions that betray our inadequacies. All of us are like that to some extent, but alcoholics and addicts are even more that way. This is so partly because they have more bad behaviors to hide but also because their grandiosity and arrogance are magnified right along with the other character defects. We need to keep reminding ourselves that alcoholics and addicts are indeed just like the rest of us—only more so. Working with addicted persons has become one of the most valuable self-learning processes I could ever have experienced. I am so very grateful to my clients for their willingness to share the exact nature of their wrongs, so that I could better see my own and the wrongs of others, including those who are not addicted but who are ready to change their lives as well.

With that as a background, I want to take you on a journey in the life of a medical professional who is a recovering alcoholic now and my dear friend. When he came to treatment many years ago he was outwardly a very nice person, friendly and personable. His wife was a wonderful lady who was very supportive of him in his profession.

To all outward appearances, they were practically perfect in every way. He had a thriving business that gave him a more than adequate income, and they were well respected by others in their hometown area. Their life was almost idyllic except for one major problem. He was a really bad alcoholic whose drinking became so serious that those he worked with finally recognized it. He came to our twenty-eight day inpatient treatment program, where he did exemplary work in the assignments, was very supportive to his fellow patients, and became a model of recovery in every way. It happened so rapidly as to appear almost miraculous. It was a textbook case of instant cure, and the treatment staff members were all very happy and proud of him. During the third week of treatment he had his family week. His wife came. She shared how serious his alcoholism had become and once again, he, and she, did exemplary work. They were indeed the poster children for recovery.

Our four-week treatment schedule required that each patient complete the first five steps of the Twelve Step program of AA. Fifth step was usually set up for the week after family week, which would then be the patient's fourth and final week of inpatient treatment. I was the one who had the place of hearing the fifth steps of each patient, and it came time for my friend to do this session.

He came to the scheduled appointment looking very respectable and calm. He brought with him several pages of neatly word-processed information that he used as the basis for his discussion. Now, fifth step says, "We admitted to God, to ourselves and another human being the exact nature of our wrongs." This is no easy task because it requires significant risk, trust, honesty, and humility. Imagine, if you will, a professional person sitting down in an office with a chaplain and coming clean about all the things he felt guilty about that he has done in his life. He had it all neatly arranged, completely in order and rationally and logically presented. He, once again, did a practically perfect assignment. But, the problem was that part of the "exact nature of his wrongs" was that he tried to appear perfect, in control, rational, logical, and organized. I tried to break through his defenses using all of the skills at my disposal that I had learned the hard way from working with recovering clients for many years. I finally asked him if that was all he had to say. He very politely and warmly said it was. So he left my office and walked calmly down the hall away from me and toward the recovery group who were his friends and fellow recovering colleagues. I felt very frustrated because I cared about him, and I knew he had not really come clean because he was still very much in control of his responses and reactions. I didn't know what to do or say. I was totally powerless to know or do anything that might help my friend become "real."

When he was about fifteen feet away, I felt the urge to call out to him and so I said, calling him by name, "Go and sin some more!" He stopped still, hunched his shoulders, turned around, totally shaken, and said, "What did you say?!" I laughed and said, "Go and sin some more—only this time learn something from it!" He walked slowly back into my office, shut the door, and talked for another forty-five minutes. Only, this time, he didn't use any word-processed notes. He didn't fall back on his carefully prepared presentation. He spoke from the heart. He was an active church member in his home town, so he knew the words I spoke were a cryptic play on words from when Jesus said in Scripture, "…go and sin **_no_** more." (John 8:11, KJV) He was very aware of what I had changed and he wanted to know why. This allowed him to take the risk of letting another human being, another man, another professional, a friend who was a minister, hear what he felt the most pain about in his life. Later, after his completion of treatment, we stayed in touch at his weekly continuing care sessions and from time to time in other ways for many years.

I wasn't the only person he became close to from his treatment experience. He learned from several on the staff in various ways and he was extremely grateful. He chose to use what was offered to him in ways that helped him become more real. This, as you know, is not an easy accomplishment. Perhaps it is even more difficult for those whom society places upon a pedestal of some sort. Physicians are called "Doctor." Ministers are called "Reverend" or "Bishop." A judge is called "Your Honor." Teachers are often called "Professor." Priests are called "Father." Their female counterparts are called "Sister." And so on. My friend and patient gave up his status and his carefully prepared presentation to become just another alcoholic wanting to get his life back into order. He did that and I am proud of him for this milestone accomplishment. He made progress in his own journey on the road to real.

We all need to "go and sin some more," not meaning to commit more wrongs but to admit and come clean about the ones we already have. We are all very much alike. Even the Bible says that "…there is no difference: For all have sinned and come short of the glory of God;" (Romans 3:22,23, KJV) Other spiritual teachers say much the same. Until we find a way to admit our sameness we will never learn about our specialness, for each of us has a unique story to tell through our life. My friend the professional finally admitted his "sin," his faults and his shortcomings; some of which had to do with his need to appear special.

We are all like that to some degree. But he admitted the exact nature of his wrongs, in a safe setting, where someone could help him process his memories and his feelings. How important is it for each of us to do the same? I remember postponing my own fifth step years before because I was afraid of what another minister would think about me, as a fellow pastor, sharing the things I had done wrong in my life. As it turned out, my fifth step went very well. The one I went to did not run away screaming but simply asked, "Anything else?" I learned to trust the process and the Higher Power in my own experience and to expect the same from and for others.

I have often remembered that day with my practically perfect patient. He did indeed, "go and sin some more" when he returned to my office, shut the door and shared from his heart instead of from his head. We "sin some more" when we really come clean about our past because it is as though we are reliving the events once again. In the retelling, the confessing; the emotions come. The feelings almost overwhelm and then when the forgiveness and acceptance are received the positive feelings make it all worthwhile. We all need to "go and sin some more" in this way, in a place where we can spiritually relive our past wrongs and find the absolution that can come only from a God who already knows our wrongs even better than we do and who helps us turn the "some" to "no." Change does not come easily. It did not for my patient and it will not be easy for any of us. But, we can never be truly real until we learn what it means to "Go and sin some more," not by actually committing more bad behaviors but in the process of admitting the wrongs we have already committed and being willing to make the necessary changes. We all need to learn how to "go and sin some more" in confession instead of in commission.

Bloom Where You Are

Learning to flourish where we are is challenging
Especially if it is not where we really desire to be
Accepting and utilizing our skills is tantamount
To having a centered and satisfying life adventure

We have to choose to make a difference
Regardless of where our heart and feet take us...
If we are to be happy and at ease in this life
Sometimes we are blessed to be where we wish

But most times we are steeped in the mundane
Of the "nitty gritty" battle between life and death
So we ask... How can I be of service...?
While giving all that we can to fulfill that question.

May we sink deep roots, grow where we are...
And anticipate the sun and rain while blossoming
May the following example of making a difference
Encourage us all in our life decisions.

Employees of a large supermarket chain were challenged by a guest speaker to put their personal signature on the job. A few weeks later, the guest speaker received a call from 19-year-old Johnny, a bagger from the supermarket where she spoke. He proudly told her he was Down syndrome and proceeded to tell his story. "At first I didn't think I could do anything special for our customers because I'm just a bagger," said Johnny. "Then I got an idea! Every day I come home and find a thought for the day." He would print it out, sign the back, and put his thought for the day in every customer's bag and say "Thanks for shopping with us." A month later, the store manager called the guest speaker to tell her about the transformation his store had gone through. Johnny's lane was three times longer than all the others—no one was willing to change; they all wanted his thought for the day. The whole store was filled with a wonderful spirit of service...and all because Johnny chose to make a difference.* Flourish where you are, and make a difference in the world with what God has given you. The grass is always greener wherever you water it.

Anonymous

Carol A Bond

Confessions on the Road to Real

"Rhonda's" Story

The name is changed, of course, but the following verbatim description is absolutely true. It's a real blessing that Rhonda wrote out her thoughts and had me write some of my responses that she wanted to think about later. Otherwise, this journey of faith during cancer treatment leading up to her eventual death would have joined the many other visits that remain undocumented. Her daughter gave permission, after Rhonda's death, for the visits we did record in part to be published. She said, "My mother was very open about her feelings during her last days and would be pleased, I believe, if her journey could be helpful to others." The following conversations are not smoothly written or corrected in any way. Rhonda came to each of our meetings with many of her questions and concerns already written out in her journal. Remember that my written responses are only those she wanted me to write out so she could study on them later.

    This will not read like a novel or even like a normal dialogue. **_Her_** words are what matter here. This journal is a record of **_her_** growth in spirit, which was very impressive indeed. Even my words, recorded here, are really hers because they are what she wanted/needed to hear and to remember. They give a window into **_her_** inner process. She is one of my very favorite people because of what she shared and also because of one special moment at the close of our last visit, shortly before she died.

Rhonda was a well-educated professional, respected by her peers and loved by her church group. As with many of us, she sometimes found it easier to relate to non-family than to those closest to her. This was one of the primary concerns she worked on during her courageous battle with crippling and disfiguring cancer. Rhonda had trouble talking because of the cancer that damaged parts of her face. This also made her very self-conscious in public. However, her choice for a meeting place was at a table in an open atrium area in a coffee shop where we would be inconspicuous and un-noticed in the crowd. I treasured her willingness to be open and honest with me during the several months when we saw each other almost every week. What follows is unaltered by me. We did not write things out at all during our first meetings, so this picks up in the middle of our process. This is a breathtaking record of spiritual growth from the inner struggles with her personal history to being able to reach out in a very wonderful way. She is one of my examples and role models for being "on the road to real."

Rhonda: *I was late—then ran into a funeral at 10th. Have been reading those from Matthew—and also—in the back of the Bible are some subjects with the verses to read that deal with them. Have had a pretty good week emotionally—I'm still wearing my "hair shirt" about guilt—but I read that if God says he forgives you—that should be it—not keep dragging it around with you.*

Cliff: God, thank you that you have forgiven me for _____. Help me to accept your gift to me and to forgive myself.

Forgiveness is <u>not</u>:

1) Excuse—we are still responsible to change.
2) Forgetting—we need to remember but not still feel guilty.

3) Blaming—I don't know whose fault it is and it doesn't really matter or help anyway.

Forgiveness is: Being willing to accept this gift and to do better, and try to help, not hurt self or others.

Rhonda: *I really want to feel forgiven—but my faith at times is not strong enough to really feel that inner peace that I think will come with forgiveness—Does this mean I haven't really accepted it by his grace and love and am not "a child of God" yet?*

Cliff: No, it doesn't mean you have not accepted his grace and, yes, you are a child of God now. Remember, children don't know a lot at birth. It takes time to grow and to learn. Be patient with yourself. Faith doesn't have to be strong. It is like the magnet in a compass which only has to be strong enough to point north. It can't pick anything up, it just knows where the real Power is and it points the way to God.

Rhonda: *I do find myself talking to God when I have had unkind thoughts or been critical of others—and it does seem to help to recognize that fault and say "I'm sorry" and try to remember not to be so quick to judge—for that is not what I'm supposed to do—but to let God handle it.*

Cliff: Good. Faith is progress, not perfection. The important word to remember is "Better." We grow, and we do better—none of us ever gets it totally right.

Rhonda: *(Name) will be coming to meet me again—be sure to let her know how much she has done for me. There have been some rough spots for she hasn't fully forgiven me but we're doing better. I still fear my death. It's sort of like a play—only when it's all over—it's all over and I'm still not fully accepting that—I guess we all have some fear of the unknown. And when people say "How are you?" I respond, "I'm fine," but inside I'm saying "I'm dying, I'm dying." But full acceptance isn't there yet.*

Do others who have come to this point feel this same way? What have they done to help themselves accept this? I want, on one hand, to know how—into what stages my illness will progress—but then again, knowing that will make it even more real—and I'm not sure I can handle that yet.

Cliff: Exactly right. I'm afraid of death also. Everyone is at some level, at some time. Even though I <u>believe</u> I still don't <u>know</u>, and these two are not the same. In a Louis L'Amour Western novel, one of the characters says: "To die is nothing. To have lived, and to be able to say, 'I was a man'—that is the thing." Everybody dies. Not everyone chooses to truly live. Death is not an option. I will die. Life is the choice—to decide to live as fully as we can each day is the best way to avoid the fear of death. God will take care of whatever comes next. All I can control at all, is my life today. (John 14, 15, 16; I Corinthians 15)

Rhonda: *I have found some interesting watching of TV on the Catholic Network. Not being Catholic I do not understand all that I see, but I do like the prayers and the thoughts that are given.*

When I have to leave the hospital will I still be able to see or visit with you? We will need to go down and read where the office is and then see if we can find it.

I'm so tired, could we call (Name) for another time? I cannot work today—will call about tomorrow.

I feel I am losing everything. I feel crazy. I feel guilty for what I am putting my family through. I feel I have lost everything—my closeness to God—my faith—everything is gone. I want to find a place, cover up my head. I'm ready to die, but insurance won't let me.

I have a teacher friend from (Name)—large family—and she thought she possibly knew you.

Do I start back at the beginning? In some ways I feel stubborn. I don't want to do anything. I feel I want someone to tell me everything to do—to bring to me—not me go out to them.

I have a terrible feeling of guilt for all the problems I'm going to cause my family, some real financial hardship because of my poor management.

I feel guilty because of the estrangement with my son, but I'm afraid to find out the reason why because I think it involves my daughter, and she will not take kindly to it. I know I annoy her, she feels she has put her life on hold because of me, and I'm going into never-never-land, leaving her with all the work.

Cliff: <u>Feelings are not facts</u>. You do have value, as a person, not as a cancer patient. You are not alone. Friends, family, and God are here. There is hope—to not feel so guilty.

Rhonda: *It seems like a long way back up the spiral. I really hurt that I do not feel close to God, and I was doing so well—I thought. I was learning to love and be loved, right now. It's still there but not close or comforting.*

Cliff: The mystics, those who spent all their waking hours in prayer, write about what they sometimes felt. They called it "the dark night of the soul," when they felt no closeness to God at all. We all have those times. It will get better.

Rhonda: *I feel abandoned by my doctor. I know he can't do any more, but I now go to someone who really doesn't know me at all—and it hurts.*

I have trouble with "love." Affection I can handle. Earlier, when I was worrying about God loving me without my full return, the song title, "There Is No Greater Love" came to me, and when I was talking, I guess to start with, suddenly the phrase "I love you" stepped into my thoughts—only that one time, but I am grateful for it.

I am so lucky that my co-workers have written to me—one wonderful woman had me in her prayers.

Do other churches, not condone—but perhaps understand suicide without one feeling eternal damnation?

Cliff: (We talked about feelings of suicide quite a bit but she wanted me to write this down for her) There is nothing God cannot forgive.

Rhonda: *We have this prayer you helped me with. I'm not too long on suffering. That bothers me as much as anything.*

(The following is a note written to her doctor)

Please write down everything my daughter should know. My cancer is terminal. The coughing keeps me very uncomfortable. I have back pain, cannot lie down because everything gets stiff. Cannot really sleep.

Everything has to go through the PEG—(feeding tube)--what would be the value? Who does that? With a machine. I don't want to prolong too much. My hospital insurance is with (Name). Do I use any of the things I have?

I am supposed to drive to (Name) in the morning. Do you think I'll be able to? I can try—I got here. What pain medicine can I take when I get home? I have a stick shift and it is very hard to use. Call my daughter and see what she says. Would you leave a message on machine saying I should not try to drive to (Name) tomorrow? No money. Please tell (Name) I was there this morning. I tried and tried to wake someone up. Please call her.

How long is the hospitalization for the trache? My mental condition is not too good. Also, right now I have an upset stomach.

(The following is a note written to her daughter)

(Name) I have a favor to ask and you probably think—now what—I've done so much, there is still more to come and she wants a favor. My favor is; help me to show you how much I really, really appreciate all you have done. It was so wonderful to come in and find everything so neat and clean and I want you to know how much I liked it.

One thing I would like to do is to be able to touch, pat, hug, sometimes when I really feel that you are doing so much—at a real sacrifice to yourself. When I look at what might have been if you had not stepped in and taken care physically of me—I really shudder when I think of what might have been, and, I'm really afraid of what lies ahead—when I am hard to get along with. That's fear speaking out.

I'm really trying to become close to God, to be able to talk with him, act in the way I should, and one thing I would like to do—touch, pat, hug. I did not grow up in a family that did that and so I've had a poor background to do that—but I've been around some people who do show physical warmth and love. I want to do that, but I have hesitated to do it with you.

So, my favor—I will be hesitant at first but I want to learn to do it. I hope it won't offend you but I do ask your permission before I start this. It is most difficult to write about. It is really hard to have to put everything into the written words.

You have faith and I'm trying to achieve it, as Chaplain Bond says, "Faith is progress, not perfection." I would like to write to you and say "thanks"—or "I'm sorry."

(The following is what I believe was her final note for physicians)

Call Dr (Name)'s office. Can I take something for this stuff in my throat—and why isn't he still my doctor? My new doctor doesn't know anything about crazy people.

When Rhonda met with me at the time of our last visit, she stopped briefly behind the chair where I was sitting as she prepared to leave. Before I rose to bid her farewell, she paused, then touched me gently on the shoulder. She had not touched me before that time. I can still feel that touch and it means a great deal.

As I reviewed the notes given to me by Rhonda's daughter after Rhonda died, I was amazed at what she felt was of most value to her. I had to chuckle at myself because I said other things that I thought were better or more profound but she did not want them written. It is an ongoing reminder to me that sometimes the client knows what they need better than I do.

I facilitated her funeral and many people came to pay their respects. I am honored that she shared, listened, and learned what she needed in preparation for her own dying. She set the agenda and she took me where she needed to go. And she did it with gratitude and with love.

Rhonda touched me in many ways. Eventually she did so in that gentle, shy, grateful touch on my shoulder shortly before she went to be with the God she wanted so much to love her. Rhonda did the work she needed to do and she asked for the help she wanted and took from that what was useful for her. As I reflect on our visits, I wish I had said some things differently, or given her a different perspective at times. But I also believe that she was the one who knew what she needed; she accomplished her goal and she did it very well. I am still very impressed with her and what she did in those brief times we had together.

Rhonda, you continue to touch me in so many ways. By asking me to write certain things out, you told me what was important to you. Perhaps those things are also important to others who are facing a similar struggle. I am grateful for what you taught me. Thank you for your time.

Suffering

Seeing old barns, windmills, the old hand pumps, aged rocks
Mesa Verde ruins and weathered buildings has its charms
But empty tumble down homes are sad with gaping wounds
One wonders at what lives were lived there…now gone

It's hard to imagine beauty in financial or emotional ruin
That so many have encountered with loss of home and job
Families uprooted, in shelters, living on the street, hunger, despair
Slums, losses and hopelessness do not feel pleasing to the senses

I wonder is there really "strength and grandeur in suffering?"
Some poet might say that but do they know firsthand?
Experiencing pain and sorrow at the time is wretched right then…
A body or mind racked by misery usually is not grand

Maybe strength and power can be gained by perseverance
Though continued agony of body or spirit wears a person down
Being stoic and persistent bearing the burden with faith
Can, if not just pretension, be inspiring and increase nobility

Maybe the dark times, storms, suffering and weathering in life
Like old barns, show character through deepened lines
The mettle and tenacity for living etched firmly in the features
With sad eyes, yet bold and knowing, from enduring and surviving

Carol A Bond

"This Is Not Good"

In spite of a hospital's best care, people still die. Not all of our patients recovered and went home to family and friends. On some floors, death is a rare situation. On other floors, death happens with some regularity. One of my assigned areas was the oncology floor, which meant a significant number of our patients would die while in the medical center. On this particular day, I was paged by the nursing staff because one of our patients had passed away and the family members were there, requesting a chaplain. Within a few moments, I arrived at the room and was ushered in by the nurse who introduced me and then left me with the family. What I saw in that room needs to be explained so you can begin to understand the strong, emotional dynamics involved when someone dies and others are left behind. We are often not well prepared for that event and this particular situation was strong evidence of that.

The room was a single-bed room. The bed was across from the door, by the window. The deceased patient was a man in his early eighties, lying on his bed, his body covered to the neck with the blankets. Standing on the far side of the bed by the window was a five-year-old boy gazing at his grand-father's face, which was about at the boy's eye level. The boy wasn't saying anything. Standing in a group, in a cluster by the door, away from the bed and the boy were five or six family members who were talking to the boy. They were trying to explain what had happened and what it meant for someone to die. They were using common metaphors for death such as "The angels came and took Grandpa away," and "It was time for him to go to his home in heaven." When I entered, some of the family members glanced at me with a look that I took to mean they could use some help with the boy. From the body language of the group, it looked like the boy was doing better than the adults because he was close to the bed while the adults were as far away from it as they could get and still be inside the room.

I walked over to where the boy was standing and stood beside him. The family waited expectantly for the chaplain to do something. I introduced myself to the boy; he told me his name and told me this was his grandfather. We talked very little for the next few minutes and I just stood close by waiting. The family members decided I wasn't going to do much after all and resumed talking quietly among themselves, still across the room from the bed, close to the door. After a few moments the boy looked up and said to me, "This is not good." That was heard by the family, who were now listening to what the boy was saying.

Now, I have been present at many bedsides during my life where someone has died. I had never heard anything more profoundly true than that. Most adults are afraid to say that out loud. We say that death is part of God's plan. We say that this was their time to go. We say they are with the Lord. While all of this is theologically true and can be a comfort as life goes on, at the moment of death there is a need for the expression of sorrow and grief. This child knew that. We adults say many things at the time of death, but this child was more honest with his feelings than we often are. He knew this wasn't a good thing, and that death means separation. His grandfather was his friend and now he was gone. "This is not good." I was impressed. Actually, I was amazed, so I just stood by the boy and paid attention.

The family members quieted down also and were watching to see what would happen next. What was the chaplain going to do now? If that was their intention, they were going to be very disappointed because once again, I listened to the boy and watched him, all the while standing close by but not actually touching him. After a few moments, he reached out and took his grandfather's hand from under the covers and raised it a few inches above the bed. The family members held their breath and I was intrigued. He dropped the hand and Grandpa's hand and arm fell, limp, onto the bed. The family gave a gasp. The boy looked up at me and said, very clearly, "He is not here." The family members stayed where they were, wide-eyed and a bit in shock. I don't blame them. I was pretty much the same although for different reasons.

After a minute or two, the boy walked over to the small table in the room at the foot of the bed and talked a few minutes with some of his family who came over and said some words to him. After a while, he took out of his pocket several Power Ranger action figures and stood them up on the table. I sat down in the other chair and watched him and listened to him as he talked through the Power Ranger figures. He had one of them say to another figure, "My Grandpa just died." The response by another Power Ranger was, "I'm sorry." The response to that was, "That's okay." And on it went for a bit. He was working through the grief process using the Power Rangers as his vehicle for expression. Wow. I have never witnessed the equal before or since. What we adults were unable to do very well, this child did exceedingly well.

So, what did the chaplain "do?" The chaplain created a safe place for that boy to say farewell to his grandpa and by my silence, encouraged the family to listen instead of talk. It is very difficult to hear when one is talking. Yes, there were words spoken to the boy and the other family members by the chaplain, but I don't remember what they were. They were pretty much the standard information that families need when a loved one dies. But the real work of spiritual healing was done by this five-year-old boy who taught us all what it means to grieve. In that situation, I understood why Jesus valued children so highly and suggested that unless we can be as little children are, we cannot comprehend the Kingdom of Heaven.

Death is not good. When someone dies, they truly are not here. We all know that, of course, but to be able to just say it without needing any explanation or sugar-coated niceties was refreshing indeed. Not only that, this chaplain learned from that child. I am still mystified by death. A person can be alive one minute and not alive the next. I am not even sure what happens or exactly when it happens, much less how it happens. I know death is real, but there is still that mystical quality that leaves me feeling very unsure and uncertain. This young child was so thoroughly connected to his grandfather that he saw immediately what had changed. I suspect it isn't the cellular death of the organism that defines death but the loss of the relationship—the loss of awareness. We are most dead when we can no longer relate or connect with others. This child didn't know biology, psychology, theology, or any of the sciences. All he knew was that a brief time before this moment he could talk with his grandfather, look into his eyes and touch him. Now that was all gone. Grandpa was truly dead because there was no longer any vital relationship. And, that was not good.

Many of us don't know what to say in the face of death. Saying something "positive" may give us comfort, but it might not be very helpful to the one feeling the loss. Actually, they might then feel obligated to respond with words of confidence or faith even though their inner spirit is crying out in pain and grief. Saying nothing is often the best thing to say. Or, perhaps to just say we are sorry. Or perhaps, what we need to do is offer a hug and hold them while they cry. There is a time to offer spiritual encouragement. But sometimes we don't allow the Spirit's sense of timing to guide us in what we do or do not say. "When in doubt as to what to say—don't" is sometimes the best advice. I didn't say much that day. I didn't need to. I was there, close by, and that child allowed me to be his comfort and his encouragement. The family allowed that also, even though that wasn't their conscious intent at first. At a time when so much was "not good," this was a very good thing indeed. I was content to just be one of this child's, and I believe, God's "Power Rangers."

Heaven

Heaven could be an interesting place
If personalities go with the person at death
There'd be jokes, humor and laughter
Music by the masters would be overwhelming
The singing would be heavenly awesome

One of our Moms would be amidst the other great songsters
The other Mom would be at the piano or organ
Yes heaven could be an interesting place
If there were no violence or harmful words
And personalities were allowed to be

Gratitude and thankfulness would overflow
What greater praise to the Creator could there be…
I'd like to think of it that way
So when those I care about sigh their last
I can think of them perfectly at ease with their talents

Carol A Bond

"Oh There You Are—I Knew You'd Find Me!"

She was a rather pleasant-looking lady in her middle eighties. She was also one of my cancer patients where I worked as a chaplain on the medical oncology floor. It was my privilege to have the opportunity of visiting with her as she received daily medication and tests while she was an inpatient. She was of German extraction but spoke excellent English so our communication was clear. As we became better acquainted, she told me how she had been one of the prisoners in the Nazi death camps during WWII. She didn't go into more detail than was needed, but she did share some of the horror of being without hope or human kindness for a long, long time. Most members of her family died of starvation or from other more brutal causes, but she survived and it was clear that she felt guilty for being alive when so many others were not.

There wasn't much that I, as a chaplain, could say directly that would bring peace to her spirit because I had absolutely no experience that came anywhere close to hers. So, I listened to her, prayed with her, held her hand from time to time, and saw her regularly on my rounds in the hospital. Over the ensuing days and weeks, we became well enough acquainted to be called friends. It was an honor to have her accept my presence as helpful to her as she faced the difficult and sometimes painful treatments for her cancer. She was remarkably grateful for the care given to her, and it pained me to realize this lovely lady, and many others like her, had been treated so badly by other people. Now, however, she was receiving compassionate and loving care by the entire treatment team at the medical center.

The time came when she was taken to surgery and then transferred to another floor to recover. As was usual, another chaplain was now the one to provide pastoral care on that unit because we worked on assigned floors, not necessarily for a particular patient. I visited with the other chaplain so she would know about my friend and a bit of her history. I was confident that good spiritual care would be provided by my colleague, and it was. My fellow chaplain enjoyed getting to know this delightful lady and visited with her during the several days she was on the post-op floor.

The day finally arrived for our patient to transfer back to the oncology floor after her recovery from surgery, and I learned about her medical progress in our morning team meeting. After that day's meeting, I went to see my friend and to resume my regular visits with her. As I walked into her room she looked up and saw me. What she said to me has become one of my most treasured memories because she said, "Oh, there you are. I knew you'd find me!" I was almost brought to tears because my mind went to her history of abandonment and loss of hope. She had not been "found" by anyone for those terrible years in the death camp. She held onto hope only because it was her nature, not because of any encouragement from her situation. She was truly a survivor, but even more than a survivor she was someone who flourished in the most difficult of settings. So, now, her joy at being "found" was authentic and wonderful to see. She trusted me to "find" her. Perhaps, as I think back on that day, this was the most profound aspect of the entire interchange. "I knew you'd find me" were words that said so much. They included her time of abandonment and they included her spiritual faith in a

God who would not ever utterly abandon her. Her words spoke of a depth of feeling that was far beyond anything I had ever experienced, and yet, they opened up my heart to sense how very significant our friendship had become to her. She, who had been overlooked as being of no value by her captors, gave me the gift of importance and value. This was beyond ordinary importance; it was truly cosmic. I found her. Yes, but for my part, she found me. The gift she gave me was beyond price, and I treasure very highly the experience of knowing her.

As she improved in health, the time came when she was to return to her home. I paid her a visit on the day she was discharged from our care, and she asked me for a blessing. I was honored and pleased to do so, and we had an emotional, spiritual farewell prayer together. I remembered that during my time at Baker University. Dr. George Wiley, my primary professor, led me in an independent study in 1978. As part of that class, he took me to a nursing home and during a visit he asked one of the residents to bless him. I had never experienced anything quite like that, and it impressed me greatly. So now, I knelt at my patient's bedside and asked her to bless me. Her face lit up until it seemed the room itself brightened when she laid her hands on my head and prayed the most wonderful prayer for me and for my ministry. I don't remember a single word she said because it was beyond phonetics.

There are moments in our life when we sense the presence of the Divine in ways that transcend ordinary time and space. This, for me, was one of those times. Yes, as chaplain I had brought the love of God into her treatment for cancer. Yes, as a fellow human being I reminded her that not all others will hurt or abandon her. All this and more happened as a result of our interaction as patient and chaplain. But, what she gave me has become a part of my core existence and will remain a part of me for the rest of my life and even forever. She taught me that many people feel abandoned. She taught me to look for that and not to assume that others feel okay. She taught me to "find" others who have their own memories of being alone and without hope. Her experience was in many ways unique, but in other ways she had the wisdom to know we all share that feeling from time to time. Some will never say the words, "There you are—I knew you'd find me!" but they will feel them when we offer ourselves to them in friendship and trust. There are many kinds of abandonment, but they can all be addressed when we take the risk of friendship. Thank you, my friend, for allowing me to be your friend and for teaching me what cannot be taught in school. But, most of all, I thank you for the blessing.

What Now

One of the laments of the mature age group
Is realizing that although we have lots of experience
We're no longer needed or particularly wanted
Age and all it has to offer is rejected in favor of youth
Despite all its inexperience…they can be trained
The older ones are real and no longer fooled
By the endless promises and pep talks
To give all for the company in hopes of receiving
A fair share, good benefits and security
We've been there, done that and know it's a sham

In the twilight years we've learned through hard knocks
And think we have much to offer in this life yet
Finding a way to refocus the energy of daily work
Whether in new avenues of employment
Or by investing personally in family and others
Or at last delving into a forgotten dream or desire
Many honored ones didn't accomplish their destiny
Until their later years and the stresses of life
Eased as children were raised and emphases changed

But, we miss being at the center of where life happens
And being the go to person…the fixer of problems
And fight passing the gauntlet on to our offspring
For they do things differently and values are different
And so we resent the changes the years have brought physically
And balk at trusting others to carry on as well
And miss being important…and feel we're fading away
For we no longer do…what our title was…so we're lost
And fail to continue to BE what we always were

God bless us "olders" and open our eyes to new roads
    Show us how to serve in our own special way
Maybe not in the arena of the work place but one to one
        With the tools we still have and the love we want to share.

Carol A Bond

Three Little Words

She was a fiery, deeply spiritual woman, and she had cancer. She also had a devoted husband who was great support, going with her to doctor appointments and attending the cancer support group I co-facilitated with a social worker. He and I are friends even to this day. She was positive in her outlook and compassionate in her interactions with the others in group. She was wonderful. But she had cancer and her particular cancer was known for spreading after lying dormant for a period of time. She knew all the facts and didn't flinch or pull punches during group. My social work co-leader and I were grateful for her involvement because it made our jobs that much easier. We could pretty much let her share with others and see the benefit her attitude and outlook made in their fight against their own cancer. Eventually, after a year or so, her cancer began to reassert itself with a vengeance and she was finally bedfast, at home, with support from visiting nurses and from her family. She could no longer attend the group and she was very much missed.

Since she couldn't attend group, I offered to visit her at the home if she and her family would want that. One day, they did ask me to come for a visit. I hadn't seen her for several weeks and during that time, the ravages of the cancer had taken their toll. I might not have recognized her if she had been one in a crowd because of the wasting of her body. But there was no wasting of her spirit. That was still vibrant and strong, even though her voice was weak.

She was propped up on pillows in her bed with her mother sitting right there by her head. I was invited to sit on the edge of the bed, which I did, carefully, holding the hand she held out to me. I was her friend and also a chaplain, so some of what we discussed had to do with her spiritual preparation for death. Actually, there wasn't a lot of talk about that because she had been prepared for death in the way that she lived. But she did want to make sure I agreed with her preparations. I did. We talked. We prayed. We sat quietly.

Then, she looked at me for a moment and with tears in her eyes she said, "Cliff, I love you!" It took me by surprise and I fumbled for an answer before saying, "Thank you." Yes, that is what I said and I wasn't even sure at the time why I said it—more about that in a minute. We visited a bit more, I said goodbye to her and to her mother, who walked me out to my car. The next day, that lovely, vivacious lady died. I attended her funeral, which was held in a great cathedral with many people in attendance. I was invited by the family to be part of the "wake" before the service in which many people shared memories and stories, some quiet and many funny and joyful. She was missed so much by so many—including me.

I thought about what happened that day in my patient's home and began to let my memories, training, beliefs, family values, and so on come into play. I was raised a Baptist. We had strict rules about familiarity with someone else's spouse. We didn't dance because that would have been too intimate with a person to whom we weren't married. We said "I love you" only to our own spouse or to our own children, or other family. Those were the rules. So, in that moment when my friend said she loved me, I was paralyzed by so many old tapes. What she said to me was nothing even remotely close to being inappropriate. My response was not "bad," but it was lacking when compared to what might have been said had I not been stricken dumb by my own inner "stuff."

Medical professionals have their code of ethics and must keep a professional distance from their patients. Mental health clinicians need those boundaries also so that healthy limits are in place to protect patient and care giver from being inappropriate. Therapists or chaplains ignore those boundaries at their own peril. That is all true. But, what would have been an appropriate response to her in that situation, that day, with her mother right there by the patient? I have thought a great deal about that and now I would say, "I love you too!" Those "three little words" have power beyond their size. They are not to be used casually, of course, but there is a time for them to be said. This was such a time and I missed an opportunity. When we tell someone we love them or are open to another person saying that they love us, something very powerful and very human, happens.

Our family has a beautiful plaque on our wall that says, "To love and be loved is the greatest joy on Eearth." We bought it years ago at a garage sale and wondered why it was priced so cheap. One day our teen aged children said, "Dad, 'earth' is misspelled." Yes, it was. ("Eearth") We hadn't noticed. Since it wasn't perfect, it was discarded by the previous owners. But, we kept it because it *was* imperfect. It was just like we were—imperfect but with the perfect message. We knew what was important. Being loved is what matters, not how one spells "earth." With my client I was hung up on what was the "right" thing to say, and so I missed the opportunity of sharing the greatest joy on "Eearth," which is to love and be loved— or in this case, to have said it. I missed the opportunity. Did I learn something from this encounter? Yes, I did and that lesson is so very important. Saying "I love you" can become a repetitious statement without much substance. But it can also be a powerful sharing from the heart. My client meant it. I meant it, too, but could not say the words at that time because of rules that were taught to me. How many of us have avoided saying the words to someone who needed to hear them? They are good words.

In my early training I was told to never meet alone with a female client in a closed room. I was taught to be very careful. Actually, the spirit of that advice is sound but is that really possible, or even helpful, every time? I have a number of colleagues who have become involved in situations that ruined their ministry when they thought they were somehow "above" that kind of temptation. So, the issue is an important one. Everything depends so much on context. What happened with my cancer patient was very different. I was caught without any way out and my old "tapes" dictated my response. I have recorded another "tape" now. When it happens again, I can say those three little words and mean them, guilt free. Being real is, well, **real**.

Love in Action

Our daughter, as a single parent, takes the parenting of her two sons very seriously. She gave me permission to share with you these particular actions she chose to take in their childhood. And, if you should happen to visit in her home, she would be likely to do the same for you. She is just that kind of spiritual person. She says:

Here are the prayers and songs I do for the boys.

Every night before I go to bed (even when the boys aren't home) I go into their rooms and say the following prayer. It's always the last thing I do before I leave the room. I guess I'm a bit OCD because if I have to go back in to their rooms, I have to say it all over again. It's like I leave the room in a protection bubble when I leave.

May God bless you and keep you safe from harm
May your dreams be pleasant and free from fear
I love you to pieces for ever
Goodnight (name, name)
This child is protected by God
I love you

I have 2 short prayers that I say as I check the doors and get ready to go to bed:

May God bless all who dwell within this house and keep us safe from harm
In Jesus name, Amen

May God bless and watch over my children
Protect them
Watch over them
And keep them safe from harm
In Jesus name, Amen

Here's the silly little song that's sung to the tune of "Jesus Loves You:"

Mommy loves you this I know
Cause I always tell you so
You're my angels
I'm your Mom
I will make you grow big and strong **(must make the muscleman pose)**
Yes Mommy loves you **(accentuate the word "you" with a poke in the belly)**
Yes Mommy loves you
Yes Mommy loves you
And I always will

Our last little silly tune:

I love you oodles
And noodles
And poodles
And gobs
I love you to pieces
I love you
Forever

Camille Bond Carson

"I Will Never Again Settle For Less"

She was an attractive woman of African American descent in her thirties, willingly and even eagerly visiting with the chaplain of Welsh, Scotch/Irish descent in his sixties, at the close of her addiction treatment experience. She was presenting her fourth and fifth step work, which involved taking a fearless moral inventory of one's self and then sharing the exact nature of her wrongs with "God, self and another human being." If you know anything about addiction, and the wrongs that can be done while under the influence of a mind-altering substance, you might understand the significance of this session. If you happen to be Roman Catholic, you might understand about the confessional but this Twelve Step program is far more specific. She could easily identify the wrongs she had done. She could hardly forget them because they bothered her greatly. They connected to powerful feelings of guilt, shame, regret, and fear of being found out. The wrongs themselves are no great mystery to anyone who has spent time listening to the stories of life from the down-and-outers or the up-and-outers. Social status has little to do with shame or guilt, especially when it comes out of an addictive experience. So, here she was, telling a minister, a pastoral counselor who worked as a chaplain on a treatment unit, things she could hardly admit to herself, much less to a man who was a stranger only a few weeks previously. So, why would she do this? Simply put, she wanted to know the "exact nature" of those wrongs, not just the wrongs themselves. She wanted to identify the negative pattern to her wrongs. As it turned out—she did do just that.

The actual content of her fifth step is, of course, confidential and is neither recorded nor reported to anyone else. That kind of absolute trust is essential in this kind of session, but it is allowed to let the treatment staff members know how well the client/patient did in her process. I could say she was specific and not vague. I could report that she was in touch with feelings and didn't just remain rational or logical. I could, and did, report that she exercised significant risk and trust as well as honesty and gratitude during her time with the chaplain. What really impressed me and made so much sense to the client was when she said, "I have settled for less too often, and I will never settle for less again."

"I will never again settle for less!"

It is not only addicts, alcoholics, gamblers, overeaters, workaholics, or their numerous kindred who settle for less. Settling for less is easy and it is usually comfortable. I do it. You do it. It's just hard to see ourselves clearly as doing it when it happens to us. I am attracted to people who are not satisfied easily, who want to go the extra mile, who give more than is required. I like to "hang out" with them and did for many years when I worked in healthcare as a clinical chaplain. I love the doctors who are exhausted and overwhelmed but take the time to listen and care. I respect the surgeons who are on their feet for hours bending over a patient whose life is literally in their hands. I admire the nurses who lovingly care for adult patients who need the same complete physical care as a newborn child. I appreciate the social worker who painstakingly makes numerous phone calls to facilitate safe discharge of a patient from the hospital. I love the chaplain who arrives at a crisis situation and stands quietly by the side of grieving family members and gives comfort and hope without seeming to really be "doing" anything. I love those and so many more like them who do not settle for less.

I hear many of my clients say "I always knew my parents loved me." What they mean is that they were not told that in so many words; neither were they held, hugged, and cherished physically very often if at all, but "they knew they were loved." It is so easy to settle for less. It is not only the obvious deficits in an addictive relationship that result in this. All too often, good people settle for less in their homes, their jobs, or in their church. My wonderful friend who was presenting her fifth step to me burned those words into my mind and my heart. "I will not settle for less!" Never again will she do that and feel okay about it. The Twelve Step Program says "Half measures avail us nothing." That is the same thing. Good enough is not good enough. It always needs to be as good as it needs to be, and that is not the same thing as good enough. "Good enough" is never good enough.

When I was a service manager in a car dealership many years ago, my mechanics would often say, "close enough isn't close enough," then someone else would say "except for hand grenades" and some wise guy would add from the back of the shop, "or atom bombs." They said a lot of other things too, all full of folk wisdom and often very humorous. But the important thing they said is backed up by what that lady said in her fifth step session which is, for all of us, "Don't settle for less!" Close enough is not good enough. It always needs to be as good as it needs to be and anything less is truly "less" and will not satisfy us, nor will it meet the needs of those we love.

Of course, reality teaches us that things don't always work out according to our plans, and sometimes settling for less is what needs to happen. But, we don't need to accept it as the final word or the end result. If you will allow me a personal reflection for a moment, there have been many plans or dreams that didn't and probably won't work out as well as desired. Sometimes things just don't work out at all like we want, so what do we do then? The personal note is that I have never had anything work out easily or go smoothly in my entire life. I hear stories about how "God just worked everything out." I am sure that happens for some, but it has not happened for me. When doors opened it was because I turned the knob, pushed, or kicked my way in. In other words, things did work out but it wasn't easy. I figure if God wants a door to be shut, it will stay shut so if it is supposed to open, it might need some encouragement or persuasion for it to swing the way it needs to swing. In the words of my client, "I will not settle for less."

One final word about this, if you please. I am not easily convinced of anything because, by nature and by experience, I am somewhat of a cynic and what I like to call a "realistic optimist." I can be fooled and have been many times. But I am a student of evidence and I believe in what works. Therefore, I will not settle for less either. I want the best, I work for the best, and I will not just accept less than what needs to happen because of an inconvenience. As a mechanic, if I build an engine for you, it will start on the first try and it will run well for a long time because I won't settle for less, or "close enough." Working with people is far more important than building an engine.

Caring for our family is of more value than getting along with strangers or looking good to people who really don't matter that much in the long term. Remember that next time your child or your grandchild asks for your time or your spouse needs you to be there for him or her. Don't settle for less. I will do my best to remember what my friend taught me that day when she taught herself, "I will NOT settle for less!" Amen to that for sure.

Attitude Adjustment

Today things seem all jumbled up
Getting up to do the same things again
Same basic routine...same face...same chores

Yet... it is a new day with vast opportunities
Decisions to be made...people to see...
Yes, chores to do and daily duties...

But then amidst my grumbling I think
A classmate is abed dying of cancer
Few choices left for this one, only closure

But I am able to do my daily work
I can go and come, do or not do
Today could indeed be a fantastic day

My attitude has had a major adjustment
Now I see the sun coming up...the moon fading
My grandchildren laughing and joking

People going to work...or walking their dogs
It doesn't matter about the dust bunnies
Or the laundry...or other chores

It's being aware and in touch each moment
Relating to others...e-mailing...encouraging
Seeing needs and helping out...it's BE-ing

I am and therefore I will Be

Carol A Bond

"I Love You to Pieces, Even If You Are a Baptist"

It has been said that truth is stranger than fiction, and I would have to agree. Sometimes events can become compelling and the human drama can become intense. In the setting of severe crisis, people will be more honest and open than they would be in normal, more ordinary life experiences.

As a hospital chaplain, I took my turn as on-call for the entire hospital. One night there was a motor vehicle accident just before midnight in which there were severe injuries and one fatality. The victims of the accident were all college students returning to their school. When the young victims arrived in our Emergency Department, all the staff members were mobilized to triage and treat them as quickly as possible. I was assigned the task of meeting family members or friends who heard about the accident and to make phone contact with those who did not know. I called the college to notify appropriate people there of what was happening and they, in turn, contacted family members of those we had in our hospital. It was a very busy time. In addition, I was to monitor the emotional and spiritual condition of those being treated.

After making an initial contact with each one, I paid particularly close attention to the young lady who was the driver of the car and who was now asking how everyone else was doing. One of her passengers had died, but she didn't know that. We were doing our best to delay telling her until family could arrive from out of town for added support. She and I visited several times during the next few hours as procedures were being done by nurses, doctors, and many others.

She continued to ask about her friends and eventually began to understand that we were being a bit evasive about giving full disclosure to her, which we feared might be more upsetting than her injuries could handle. In the course of my visits with her, I found out about her family and other details of her life as a way of getting to know her and keeping her mind off of the accident. She asked similar questions of me so that during the next few hours we ended up knowing a lot about each other. One of the items we discussed was that she was Catholic and I was Baptist. Finally, she motioned to me from her treatment room and said, "I know you are a pastor and so you can't lie to me. Did my friend die? You have to tell me."

I assessed her condition and then weighed the risks of telling her against the risks of not telling her and having her become even more upset. So, I told her that yes, her friend had died. She was quiet for a moment, cried a bit and said she figured that was what happened. I told the medical staff that I felt it had been necessary to tell her about the death of her friend, and they agreed it had been a long time to withhold that information. Nobody had yet arrived from the college or from any of the parent's homes, which was not terribly surprising given the time of night that we were making our calls.

Eventually family and school officials began to arrive and the patients were all stable enough to be transported to other facilities for specialized care. I said my farewell to the students, had a few prayers, and waited for the helicopter to come and take our patients away. As my friend was being wheeled out on the gurney, surrounded by family, she motioned me over to her side. She reached out and took my hand in hers, squeezed it and said, "I love you to pieces, even if you are a Baptist." At that moment, between us, there were no religious barriers at all. Our staff had ministered to her needs with compassion, and I had been part of that team effort. She had received what she needed in medical, spiritual, and emotional care and the religious categories that so often separate people were swept away. They didn't even exist.

As a youngster growing up in the fifties, I was told not to date any Catholic girls. I was warned about even attending church services there because of the many differences between us and them. Of course, others who grew up Catholic during that time were told the same thing about us, so understanding and communication about our religious faith were very limited. We were not to associate at a religious level and that was that. In the years since then, many of the boundaries and suspicions have softened somewhat but for many, there is still uncertainty about just how far we can be in fellowship without crossing whatever "line" there may be. Prejudice is an ugly dynamic and it can prevent any of us from thinking clearly. It is an ailment we all suffer from to some extent, so it's important when those moments of clarity come and sweep it away. Such a moment came for a Seventh Day Baptist chaplain and a Roman Catholic student in a Sisters of Charity of Leavenworth hospital ER during the wee hours of the morning. Clarity is priceless.

As a chaplain, I've asked for assistance from Catholic Priests, Jewish Rabbis, Jehovah Witness Elders, Mormon Elders, and Bible Church Pastors. I have prayed with Hindu patients before surgery and supported Atheists or Agnostics in their worry about family members. I've facilitated the burning of sage for Native American patients and comforted Wiccan adherents in their anxiety. The freedom that comes with being a chaplain is a priceless gift, but also a significant responsibility. Crisis is a great leveler. Military chaplains and police chaplains know this as they provide spiritual care across religious boundaries that would be difficult to breach in other situations.

In our Christian Faith we sometimes forget that Jesus was a Jew. What he taught was consistent with the Old Testament prophets in whose shoes he walked. Jonah preached repentance to Assyria. Daniel provided spiritual guidance to Babylon. Elijah anointed kings over foreign lands. Elisha healed a Syrian military leader. Spiritual beliefs were important to Jesus but religious barriers were not. My friend and I in the ER shared spiritual beliefs even though our religious traditions were different. I prefer the spiritual beliefs to the religious traditions in times of crisis, and I know that my friend, that very scary night, did as well.

Religious beliefs are important because they provide a framework for our spiritual faith and its expression. Any person who cares about the welfare of another human being is on the same spiritual wavelength. Religious differences are important and need to be respected. But when it comes right down to it, when the issue is life or death and someone is in need of human kindness and spiritual ministry, the labels cease to have importance and the differences are overcome by the common desire to love and serve our neighbor as we do ourselves. I can work with anyone who shares that belief. I was blessed by a frightened and grieving college student young enough to be my granddaughter. She was blessed by a chaplain who was not of her particular religious background but who was concerned about her welfare and could be trusted to tell her the truth and then stand by her as she dealt with the emotions that came from knowing that truth. Anything less would be a denial of my call by God to become a pastor in the first place and a violation of my ordination as a minister of the Gospel. It was a good night—a night to remember.

Hugh Prather says:

(From <u>Notes to Myself—My Struggle to become a person</u>)

"One thing has become quite clear:
all acquaintances are passing. Therefore, I want to make the most of every contact. I want to quickly get close to the people I meet because my experience has shown we won't be together long."

Realistic Hope

Part of becoming a real person is having the ability to have hope and to help others find hope as well. I became very aware of that as I worked as part of the hospital oncology support team for fourteen years. Cancer was perceived, even during my work in a hospital into the early twenty-first century, as a dark and deadly disease that promoted despair in the hearts of patients and their families. Therefore, part of the agenda for those in health care was to help our clients find hope. We were upbeat. We were positive. We were caring. We were not "doom and gloom" as we ministered to their needs.

And yet, every patient of every doctor will eventually die of something in spite of the best care. That doesn't signal failure. That doesn't automatically signal that hope is lost. We are born, we grow, we mature, we decline, and we die. That is reality, so just what does it mean to give hope? For what do we hope? Short term, we hope to "get well" from whatever is troubling us and that is often done in a medical center. We have reason to hope for recovery from many illnesses that weren't treatable years ago. Our tools and technologies do offer hope, and the hospital staff all contributed to the offering of that hope. The goal, then, would be to intervene in premature, preventable death. But, once again, does that mean that every person will "get well?" No, of course it doesn't. So, what does it mean to offer hope?

My patients knew I wouldn't lie to them, that I would tell them the truth. That didn't mean I would tell them every fact I knew or suspected at the time they wanted information. Truth telling is not the same as reporting facts because timing and appropriate content are part of telling the truth and the offering of hope. So, how can a person have hope after they find out their disease is not going to be healed and that they are likely to die sooner than they would want? How can a medical team tell the truth and still offer hope in EVERY situation? It is not a simple question and there is not a simple answer.

What I did come to believe and share with others was what I called "Realistic Hope." If you can imagine the word "HOPE" spelled vertically and then use each letter to form a word, I shared with others that HOPE consisted of Honesty, Openness, Purpose/Plan, and Encouragement. That is what I tried to do with my patients. I wouldn't say that "I know you will be okay" because that isn't realistic at all. But, neither would I say to a patient that their cancer was untreatable and they would surely die. I would be honest and say that I didn't know, that nobody has an expiration date stamped on their body somewhere since there are "X factors" of healing that come into play, which are not totally understood. Things like positive attitude, having a purpose, prayer, diet, etc., are all factors not always of a scientific nature but which still affect a person's health and recovery even from cancer.

Statistics are often quoted that say a person with a particular type of cancer has, for example, an eighty percent chance of recovery. But, in each, individual case, those averages mean nothing. If someone is in the eighty percent group then their chances of recovery are one hundred percent, and if they are in the twenty percent group their chances are also one hundred percent but in this case, not to survive.

Each person is an individual, and we don't know what the outcome will be. So, I would encourage them and give them hope by being honest, open and purposeful. I didn't have to give false hope even though it was what I wanted to do at times. Elsewhere in this book is the story of a lovely lady who fought her cancer right down to the end. She never lost hope. As a matter of fact, "hope" is sometimes confused with "wish" and we can get way off course if we do not know the difference.

I have been in patient's rooms where a family member will say, "We are praying for you so we know you will be just fine." That is really not a helpful (or hopeful) thing to say. Prayer does not guarantee that a person will recover physically. In addition to that, if the person being prayed for doesn't recover, they often feel it is their fault, that they did not have enough faith, because others "were praying for them to get well." Death is very hard to accept but it is, paradoxically, a part of life. According to the Bible, death is the "last enemy" which will be destroyed in the future. (I Corinthians 15:26, KJV) It is very much with us now. Yes, I would like to be able to guarantee that a person will get well, recover and beat cancer because I want them to do so. I want every patient to get well. I will work in any way I can to be part of that healing journey, but I must also be realistic.

My journey to real includes the reality of sickness, accident, and death. I have to accept what is real, but I do not have to like it or cooperate with it. I've said it before and I will say it again: I pray for "the serenity to accept the things I cannot change and the courage to change the things I cannot accept" and only then to pray for wisdom to know the difference. My hope is realistic and my acceptance is active, not passive. I will change what I can. I will offer hope, and there are times when patients would literally hold onto me and not want to let go. They wanted to have realistic hope. It was more than a positive thought or a nice wish. They wanted something real.

I believe there is a way to beat cancer. I believe and "hope" that it will be soon. Completely beat it as has been done with polio. That is realistic hope. In the movie "Galaxy Quest" the hero says, "Never give up—never surrender." It is a funny movie but that line isn't humorous at all. That is realistic hope said in a different format. In a theological format, it is the Easter Sermon titled, "It's Friday—but Sunday's coming!" Death is part of life but life is stronger than death when we choose to live. Yes, that takes faith as well as hope but that is also part of love. Again, Scripture says the three that survive and endure are "faith, hope and love." (I Corinthians 13:13, NIV) Now, THAT is what I'm talking about! Realistic hope, if it is really hope and if it is really real, will have all three of those components. That kind of hope can change the course of a disease even as intimidating as cancer. I am old enough to remember polio wards where people were in iron lungs. My parents remember tuberculosis wards. We don't have either one now. Someone never gave up hope and gave us realistic hope instead.

Honesty, Openness, Purpose/Plan, Encouragement—sharing that with others in crisis is far better than offering false hope even if it is clothed in religious or medical clothing. True faith and realistic hope are very close to being the same thing. Don't settle for less. My patients taught me that. And if you want religious or spiritual terminology, I also believe realistic hope is *precisely* God's will.

Power

Each of us is just one little grain of sand
In the sea and shore of little grains of sand
Tumbling and rolling with tides or wind
Rolling and bumping against obstacles

Big rocks grate, rubble grinds and water erodes
As we tumble through the days and nights
Singly we seem to have little purpose
Together we form impressive beaches

We're often tossed about by waves and wind
Looking always to find the right place and safety
How can a speck expect to be heard in the din
Even by the Creator of sand, sky and nature?

We are at the whim of higher forces it seems
Big pebbles that grind us down fine and small
Convince us we're unimportant and powerless
Not realizing they're just an inflated, unscathed us

They don't know that united we form cement or
Bring joy in a sandbox…and safety on ice
Even one grain of sand in a shoe causes torment
Life hasn't humbled and molded them yet

Our power comes in being who and what we are
Grains of sand on many beaches doing our jobs
Called to fill many niches in this great world
Standing firm when needed and serving well

Carol A Bond

Learning From a Lady

She wasn't old or young, tall or short, rich or poor. She was, in fact, quite ordinary in a very pleasant way. She was gracious, deeply spiritual, and she had serious cancer. Her family was supportive and she had her Orthodox Faith to feed her spirit as her body was subjected to heavy doses of chemotherapy. She became my friend and although she died, I would never say she lost her battle with cancer. Neither would she.

When she was told her disease had spread, she was at first devastated and then became angry enough at the cancer to demand a second opinion. As a result, she had surgery and later went to the National Institute of Health (NIH) for state-of-the-art chemotherapy. During this time, we kept in touch by using e-mail, which worked very well. Up until that time I had never been particularly fond of this method of communication because it seemed impersonal. What I discovered is that this type of contact allows both parties opportunity to respond at a convenient time rather than being caught by an incoming phone call that demands immediate response, ready or not. Also, I have a written transcript of our conversations, portions of which have, with her permission and blessing, been used in various workshops as a powerful teaching aid. I don't believe she ever fully realized the power of her words which so eloquently describe the journey through cancer treatment that only another cancer survivor or their support persons could adequately appreciate.

A portion of our e-mail conversations, unedited by me except for disguising names, follows.

Sent: Tuesday, March 22
To: Clifford Bond;
Subject: greetings from NIH

Hi!

I arrived Sunday, had some tests done; Monday had an EKG and talked with the doctors. I was accepted for the trial, and admitted as an in-patient Monday afternoon. The doctors are so great and don't mind my incessant questions!... talked with a resident last night who is doing research on the trial - he was very interesting. My trial nurse is so nice. She stops by just to say hello and visit before she goes home... I am hoping some of these people will move to Kansas.... we have been comparing the cost of real estate. I took the pill this AM (just one this week, then starting next week, will take them daily) then had blood draws done frequently to follow how much is in my blood, how long it takes and how long it stays.

This afternoon, the blood draws became less frequent, so I had a chance to take a walk around the 300 acre NIH campus. The highlight was visiting the National Library of Medicine, the largest medical library in the world! There is much to see in the clinical center - part of it is very new, completed last fall. I should be finished with the last blood test on Thursday evening, so Friday, I hope to get a pass and take the Metro to Wash. D.C. for a quick look at the monuments, etc. Yes, the farm girl goes to the city, and takes the Metro! I have been getting tips from the nurses and studied the map... I think I can do it.

L, I talked to S after I left the voice mail, and the info I needed from Dr. G has been taken care of.

Tell Doc, T, K that all is going great. Thanks for all your help.

If you see A, tell her and the nurses on 3 as well. My trial nurse told me that this drug has been studied for multiple myeloma and is in phase III - hopefully going for approval before long. It has also been studied in other trials for other cancers, so it is not like this trial is the pioneer. That's good.

Thank you for all your help, support and prayers,

P

She had been coming to our "Learning to Live with Cancer" oncology support group on a regular basis when her health allowed. We talked about her attitude that had been instilled by family and society. She had incorporated what she heard as "Be a nice person," "don't make trouble," "do not be angry," and "always do what you should." This wasn't working for her as she faced a "guarded prognosis." So, we talked about the movie "The Ghost and the Darkness" with Val Kilmer and Michael Douglas, two actors she could show interest in. Michael Douglas' character said at one point in the film about two killer lions that were terrorizing and killing many people, "They are only lions!" What did it mean to say "Only lions?" All Pat had was cancer and "it was only cancer." She understood. In no way were we minimizing cancer. What we were doing was facing the "ghost," facing the "darkness," and we were going to find a way to confront it. Would it kill her? Perhaps it would, but she made a choice to name her fears and call them out of her own inner darkness into the light. In order to do this, she had to look at the passive behaviors she was taught and choose to learn a new attitude.

We also talked about other faith traditions and their teaching about illness, cancer and death. She shared with me some of her Orthodox liturgies as we came to Christmas and then to Easter. I found her faith to be vibrant, alive, and very useful to her as she faced her "lions." I also found myself profoundly moved as I read litanies that I as a Baptist had never experienced during the holy days of Christmas and Easter. It was really a question of which person was helping the other; and, of course, the answer was "yes." We helped each other.

> *From: Clifford Bond*
> *Sent: Wednesday, March 23,*
> *Hi*
>
> *I am so glad you have this opportunity to let the cancer know you mean business and that there is no quit in you. Even cancer feels fear in the face of faith. Magic is not what I mean, and anyway, magic is not nearly as powerful as realistic faith that confronts and accepts life, both at the same time. I will let A know and the 3 Onc nurses who will be very happy to hear about you. What they are doing out there sounds just right and I am pleased that they are doing this for you. You can tell them, if you want, that this Oncology Chaplain thanks them for what they are doing to combat your disease and to give you hope when some would just give up and accept what can be changed and allow cancer to win. Cancer can just go back to its evil source! It came from*

there, and it can jolly well just go back. In any case, you have already won the war, it is just each little battle that is in question, not the outcome. This is Holy Week and we know the "rest of the story."

You shared your church's faith tradition with me last Easter and I am reading it again. So, for now, just remember that the Easter message is, simply, "It's Friday, but Sunday's coming!!" May you continue to experience the Sunday of hope out there in that place of power. Carol did research on that area where the whole capitol complex is located and found that the Native Americans have always seen that area as a nexus of spiritual power. It still is, and as I remember our tour of the monuments I could feel it. You are precisely where you need to be, doing exactly what you need to be doing. Cool!

Take care my friend and may God bless you and curse the cancer.

Peace and joy and love, Cliff

From: P
Sent: Wednesday, March 23
To: Clifford Bond
Subject: Thanks

Dear cliff;

It was so good to hear your roar from the grandstands this AM!! I don't know if you realize how much it helps to have your realistic view of death/CA and at the same time, your wild and crazy optimism/faith/denial of CA's winning.

I will tell my doctors and nurses thank you from my friend and CA chaplain. It is an amazing place. I am so thankful to God that I am here.

It is raining outside today. My room is on the 12th floor, and I have the window spot. At night I look out over the city lights, and by day, I watch people and cars - wish I had my binoculars! Ok, I had better remember to pray for the people within this view. I wonder if the lights I see far away to the south are close to the capitol and other bldgs. I do need to pray, though, for these doctors and researchers, and the patients who are here. They are going to beat CA some day. My wing is all CA, however, there are patients here at the clinical center who have many different health probs.

It is so interesting to find out that this area was a holy place for the Indians. What was Carol's initiative to do that research? Your trip here last summer?

Will talk to you later.

P

In the process of our e-mailing back and forth we discussed Ursula Le Guin's <u>Earthsea Trilogy</u> in which the central character, the wizard Ged, says the secret to true magic is "Do the next thing." This was very profound and simple philosophy that resonated with P as she found herself facing a series of life changes which were beginning to overwhelm her if she allowed her guard to come down. What I did was to share what made sense to her at the time, and what seemed to meet the need at the moment. Part of what happened is that normalizing her life was important especially out on the Eastern Seaboard where she knew nobody. The decision we made together was to keep her up to date on my own family's activities in addition to information from her own family and her church. With her, it seemed to help in keeping better balance and perspective. This might not have worked with some others and the same is true with other approaches that were successful with P but would not connect in all situations. P was able to let me know what worked and what did not, so we could change approaches as needed.

From: Clifford Bond
Sent: March 25 2:40 PM
To: P
Subject: RE: thanks.

P,

Here it is Good Friday when I remember your sharing the Orthodox Faith Perspective on the season. I still treasure that. I think of those words and I combine them in my mind with my favorite "sermon" at Easter I ever heard and that of course was "It's Friday-----but Sunday's coming!" My church emphasized the resurrection so much that they were uncomfortable with Good Friday. Others emphasize the death of Christ so much that the new life in Christ in minimized. I like the balance.

This weekend Carol and I will go to Council Bluffs, Iowa to be with our oldest son and his family. Our daughter and her two sons, that Carol babysits, will be there also. We will take our travel trailer and camp in Craig's back yard. This will be fun for the grandchildren and for the grandparents. Enjoy your time to think, reflect, rebuke the enemy and live each day as the victory it truly is. God bless you, my friend.

From: "Clifford Bond"
To: P
Subject: Post Easter Update
Date: 28 Mar 09:48

Hi P,

    I really enjoyed the church service. We visited our oldest son, Craig, in Council Bluffs, IA over Easter weekend. We attended their Presbyterian church and enjoyed the sermon, titled "Easter is a Joke!" and the brass ensemble that accompanied the choir numbers and the bell choir that started the service. I feel fed, spiritually. Oh yes, the "Easter is a Joke" thing needs explaining. Pastor explained that Greek plays were either comedies or tragedies. Comedies were not necessarily funny as we think of it, but were stories that started with problems but turned out alright. Tragedies ended badly. So, for them, a "joke" meant a story that looked really bad for awhile but came out surprisingly well. So, Easter is truly a joke. It was well done and was shared, not read from a manuscript. It was inter relational and personal.

    Oh yes, about the DC area being holy to the Native Americans. That entire river tidal basin was not lived in by the American Indians, but visited for hunting or ceremonial purposes much like the Ouray, Colorado canyon or what is now the State of Kentucky. Native Americans had many areas that were sacred, meaning not to be lived in permanently, but visited for special reasons. Carol did the research on this to find out. We have found, in our travels, several places that are places of power, where positive energy seems to focus. The Big Horn Mountains in Wyoming, Mesa Verde, Canyon De

Chelly, Council Grove, Council Bluffs and other places have a long history of gatherings of people for important decisions. It is an interesting fact that many churches are built upon the ruins of much older places of worship, often several older places of worship from several cultures over many centuries or millennia. Holy places are just that; holy places regardless of which religion claims them for a time. So, you are in a place of power in our culture, the center of power, actually. But the roots of that power go much farther back than 1776. You are truly exactly where you need to be. If you have time, and the inclination to do so, go on line and do a search for Iroquois Nation, or Native American Worship, or History of Washington, DC and see what you find. In any case, the healing focus could not be better than there.

    Gotta run.

Take care, Cliff

From: P
Sent: Monday, March 28
To: Clifford Bond

Dear Cliff;
    Glad that you had a good Easter. It is always nice to come home from church with a full spirit. Don't you love it when you hear a sermon and it is just what you've been thinking about or experiencing?
    I laughed at the jokes that you sent to me; now I am doling them out, a few at a time, to my friends. We need more jokes!

I had a great week - fun, interesting, learning - and now I am home, taking CC-5013 daily. I was worried this AM. God, the possible side effects could be bad. Could keep me from continuing its use. What if it doesn't do anything for me. God, carry me through this. He has provided everything that I need so far. Let's just think about today, I can do today. (In the past week, I said the words many times, "do the next thing".)

I will do some research on the spiritual places/history. Sounds very interesting. I have been to some of the places that you mentioned.

See you soon,

P

From: P
Sent: April 06, 1:41 PM
To: Clifford Bond
Subject: living will

Hi Cliff;

Do you have a form for living wills? After all the Terri Schiavo news, it seems like a DPA is only part of the needed documents.

I will be at the hospital on Friday.... I am now going to the oncology floor at 11:00, then at 1:00, I am doing some typing for the Director - down in the basement. I will pop by the chaplains' office.

So far, so good with the drug. I am going back to MD for an appointment on Monday.

Maybe I will see you Friday,

your friend,

P

From: Clifford Bond
Sent: April 06, 1:49 PM
To: P)
Cc: Chaplain (Name), Chaplain (Name)
Subject: RE: living will

P,

I just happened to be at the computer. (A God thing?) Anyway, there are Living Will forms on the wall outside the Spiritual Care office on 5th floor, north hall, room 7. I will not be here Friday, so regrettably I will not see you. Talk to Chaplain (Name) if you have questions Friday. He will be here in the morning, but not in the afternoon. If you are not here in the morning, Chaplain (Name) can help you in the afternoon, after 1:00.

Glad to hear the new drug is matching up well with you. I will be very interested to hear what MD says to you Monday. Welcome back to Kansas!

Take care my good friend,

Cliff

From: P
Sent: April 29, 3:20 PM
To: Clifford Bond
Subject: looks good....

Dear Cliff;

I had an appointment at NIH on the 23rd. My CEA is dropping! Of course, they are cautious, because these are numbers and the CT in May will tell us much more, but you know my numbers have been an accurate indicator for me. My CEA on 3/21 was 76.9, on 4/25 it was 59.2 And the double excitement is the benefit to my health, plus the possibility of another drug for many people.

I arrived home Tuesday PM, very tired. I stayed with friends in Alexandria, VA, which was wonderful. But taking the bus and Metro to NIH Monday AM took 1 1/2 hours! On the way back to their apt., (well, I did have to backtrack to a missed station) it took me two hours. So on the night before and after appointments at the NIH, I will stay at a hotel and take the shuttle, delivering me to the clinic door in less than ten minutes.

Next month, I am planning to take my 15 year old son. We will go early, stay with the friends, go sightseeing for two days, then check into the hotel while I go to my appointments. It will be so much fun to take him. He is interested in many things.

This Sunday is our Orthodox Pascha (Easter), and this is Holy Week. Last night was the reading of the "Passion Gospels". Tonight is the "Lamentations of the Mother of God". Thankfully, we have the words to read silently as the choir sings, because the lines are so beautiful, heartbreaking, loving,... Last night, I was struck by the lines about the thief on the cross. He was the first to enter paradise. Isn't that amazing? A guilty man, a sinner. And yet, he was the first to enter Paradise. And how can I judge anyone, especially my brothers and sisters in Christ, my friends and parents, when Jesus took with him a man who was certainly guilty. Tomorrow is the day that we all wait for. Pascha

service starts at 10 PM and I can't begin to describe it to you!

I did not volunteer today, but maybe I will see you next Friday. Your friend, P

It was in June, just prior to P's death, that I approached her and asked her permission to use the e-mail records from her cancer treatment experience. A few of them were shared here and others were presented to a continuing education Grand Rounds workshop for nurses, social workers, and chaplains. The effect of her honesty and openness was profound on those in attendance. In August of that year, P's condition worsened to the extent that she needed hospice care. Her family gathered at the bedside; her priest came and administered the appropriate sacraments and I came for a visit, had a prayer, and sat at the bedside holding her hand as the family expressed their thanks for the help I had given their wife/mother/daughter/sister. It struck me then, and continues to impress me, that the help was mutual. P is not alone in the group of teachers in my life that I encountered during my work with cancer patients. She did not merely *accept* my sometimes admittedly sideways approach to pastoral care, she actually *encouraged* it.

What did I learn from this lady? She taught me the courage to be myself even if that flies in the face of accepted doctrine. She encouraged me to be honest and open in my own "faithing" process (I do think of faith as a verb.) She reminded me that faith is more than rules to be observed and belief is more than thoughts to be examined. Faith ("faithing") is how we behave because of what we believe because belief and behavior are essentially linked together. She celebrated the opportunity to develop an attitude, specifically about her cancer. She created her own "Oh no you don't—not today—not here—not now" confrontation toward her disease and I love her for it. She developed the attitude of refusing to ever let cancer win and, because of this attitude, didn't lose her battle with cancer. She did die of cancer, true. If we live long enough we will die of something because everybody dies. But not everybody chooses to live. Some will just exist and hope things work out. This was not so with P. She learned and then she taught that life is far too important to take for granted—or to take too seriously. After all, "it was only cancer!"

Before P died, I asked her to write out what gave her hope. Here is what she said, and I have her permission to share it. I find it absolutely inspired.

Trust in God, to whatever degree I am able.
Consistent hope from someone. The doctor needs to be that, also. Not false hope or manufactured optimism. All stages of cancer have been healed—I can be one of those.

I need to know on days when my hope is low, that there are others who do have hope for me.

Learning that the body and mind are a unit. Learning that "when my soul is healed, my body will follow."

Taking a very active role in my care and treatment. Making the decisions, asking many questions, learning to be my own advocate.

A relationship with my doctor. Telling him or her about my family, hopes, fear, etc. Giving the doctor a hug. Getting a hug. Being able to express to the doctor my frustration, anger, question their decisions and ask for a second opinion without fear of rejection or worry I will hurt their feelings!!! Being able to tell the doctor during a busy schedule (without apology) "I need your time and attention or I will die." Knowing my doctor truly cares about me and is with me through thick and thin.

Having a few close people (not just one) with whom I can be very honest. Those I can call and they make time for me. People who I don't have to support.

Having all the staff in the cancer center show genuine care about me. That means so much. All the doctors, nurses, receptionists excited when I have good news. They are an important part of my support team. Nurses and aides who cared for me months earlier during my stay in the hospital have recognized me, asked how I was, encouraged me.

Calling the nurses at the cancer center to tell of a side effect or possible problem without feeling like I'm inconveniencing them or the concern is unwarranted. They are very helpful.

You have helped me so much, through much bad news and rejoicing with me in the changes as I grow, the good news when it comes, and our talks.

Thank you so much. You are one of the many answers to prayer God has sent.

Your friend, P

Loving Others

Hugh Prather in "Notes to Myself" says:

"Love unites the part with the whole.
Love unites me with the world and with myself.
My life work could well be love.
Love is the universe complete.
Detachment is the universe divided.
Detachment divides me from myself and from others.
Love is the vision that can see all as one and one as all:
'I and my Father are one.'
Is there but one reality and one truth?
Love shows me where all minds and essences unite.
How do I get love? I have it.
I must drop my definitions of love.
Love is not saying nice things to people or smiling or doing good deeds.
Love is love. Don't strive for love, be it.
I love because I love."

May you love those you see for just being who they are...
      May you respect their travails and their journey
May you open their hearts to the music of their soul
      Have a good day my love!

Carol A Bond

"I Promise You..."

She was one of my very favorite people and a very wonderful nurse. She was a lady who was in her early 50's. She and her husband had a marvelous marriage, and her peers respected her while her patients loved her. She just had that gift for caring that makes a person feel safe and completely comfortable even during the invasive and sometimes unpleasant aspects of patient care. Anyone who has ever been a patient knows how important the nurse can be. She was an absolute jewel.

She developed cancer. It wasn't just any kind of cancer but one that was fast growing and for which there was not a dependable cure. Statistically, her days were numbered in months, not years. She knew this because she was an oncology nurse and had cared for women with the very same diagnosis, and so she could have been very despondent and discouraged. She was scared, and she was anxious but she was also a joy to visit and so, selfishly, I made sure I saw her regularly. I was good for her and her husband but she was also good for me as well.

Now, I really hate cancer and what it can do. My grandfather died of metastatic prostate cancer when I was fifteen. I had a cousin whose leg was amputated because of some kind of cancer; I never knew what "brand" it was. All I knew was that he was a few years older than I, and he had crutches because one leg was missing. Then, years later my mother was diagnosed with lung cancer even though she never smoked. There were metastases to her intestines, so she had several surgeries to prevent bowel blockage. She died of her cancer on Christmas Day, 1989, just a few months before my first grandson was born. I would have liked it if she could have seen and held him. I don't like cancer.

So, almost every day I would stop by this nurse's room, usually to find her husband sitting in a chair close by, sometimes with the patient asleep, sometimes with the husband asleep, and sometimes with them both awake. We talked, we visited, we prayed because she was a woman of strong faith in God. Some tears were shed at times, and we kept informed about what was being done by the medical team. Finally, the doctor decided that we had done as much as we could here and plans were made to send her to MD Anderson Cancer Center in Texas. She was obviously afraid to go and that mystified me because her faith and her general attitude were usually rather fearless. She did not, or would not, tell me why she was afraid. I thought it might be because it was a strange place, or that her family would not be close by. But, I was wrong.

Nurses are an interesting kind of person. Don't get me wrong, I respect and love them. My wife is a nurse and I worked with nurses for many years. But they are special. Finally, her co-workers came to me and told me what they thought was going on and wanted me to help her. Now I had some direction and a reason to be a bit more assertive in finding out the reason for her fear. I went into the room to find her awake and rather tense. Her husband was sitting at the foot of her bed, obviously distressed. I took a chair right up by her head and sat back preparing for a visit, hopefully to help her with her fear. She wasn't speaking loudly because she was rather weak, and so I stood up and leaned fairly close to her as we visited. Abruptly, she reached up, took hold of my suit jacket lapels and pulled me down close to her face and said, "Promise me that I will be strong enough to go through this!" She was not afraid of the treatments, or the place, or anything like that. She didn't want to be weak and be unable to do what she needed to do. She didn't want to let us down, her doctor down, her family down. And so I said, with her hanging onto my coat with all her strength, looking me right in the eye, "As God is my witness, I promise you that you will be strong enough!" She relaxed, leaned back and said, "I will hold you to that!" Then she let go of my coat lapels. Her husband was relieved but now, I was really scared. I spoke without hesitation but what had I done? How could I dare promise her that, and I even brought God into the promise!

I pride myself in always being honest with my patients. They always knew that if they asked me anything about their care, their prognosis, or anything at all, I would be honest with them based on what I knew. I might avoid some issues but if I said it, they knew I meant it. They trusted that. Now, I had not just given information, I had made a promise I might not be able to keep. But, it was said, she was satisfied, and she was now peaceful. I went up to the pastoral care office and shared what I had said and done. My peers listened and said, "It sounds good to us!" That helped, but I was still nervous.

She did go to MD Anderson, and she did do well, and she did come back to the hospital where I saw her for several months during which time she did well before passing quietly away. Later, her husband came by regularly to say to the staff how much he appreciated the hope that we gave her during her time there. So it worked out all right, but there is an important lesson here. Telling the truth sometimes involves taking a risk into the unknown. If all we ever do is play safe, we are not giving hope at all. Faith, according to the biblical definition, is "the substance of things hoped for, the evidence of things not seen." (Hebrews 11:1, KJV) Hope and faith are here interwoven in a tapestry of the unknown. In effect, there was a transfer of fear and anxiety from her to me. I like that. I am also willing to do that as part of my identity as chaplain. I wasn't the source of her hope but I was the conduit, the connection, the way out. But, also, this was not an automatic "I know you will be fine because I am praying for you." The timing was right. The relationship was right. And it was said under God's leading, not my own desire to say something "nice." She did hold me to that promise, and I found myself praying every day for her strength during her stay in Texas. I took it seriously and I took it personally and so did she. She reached out for a personal guarantee, not a professional one. She wanted to trust a relationship not just a medical opinion, or even a religious one. The promise was made and that promise became her strength. Promises are like that. I *promise* you this is so.

Duty

A new day after a short evening shower
The air is cleansed and fresh
Plants of all kinds enlivened
A brand new day to start afresh
The first footprints across the day
Where will they lead us…

Down the path of duty we go
Making decisions constantly
The minutes ticking by…do we notice?
Visits made, meetings attended
Too often plodding along head down
Not seeing the beauty along the way

The expectant faces, the smiles
Taking no time for little oasis breaks
Wondering why the tension builds
"I am relaxed" we say as neck muscles bunch
Even too much good can cause ill
Where is that serene place within?

To center, focus and meditate
Forget the trappings and keep it simple
Thinking of one thing at a time slows us
Quiets the mind and in silence…we can listen
Was life experienced today--or endured?
The choice is ours to make….

Carol A Bond

"You Are Forgiven"

In 1989, we had a very cold winter where we lived in Topeka, Kansas. However, more than the weather made it a "cold" wintertime because on Thanksgiving Day that year, Carol's paternal grandmother died. Carol had been very close to Grandma during the years on the farm when Carol spent many overnights with her and helped with farm chores. Now, Grandma was gone and it was a time of deep sorrow. During the same time, my mother was fighting her battle with terminal cancer and was rapidly declining.

Carol and I made numerous trips to Nortonville, Kansas, on the cold and snowy roads that December, sometimes one of us alone, and sometimes together. We kept vigil and all of us "children," including spouses, were there with my father who continued to be the primary caregiver for Mom. My sister who was next oldest to me came with her pastor husband from New York State, and our youngest sister came with her husband from Kansas City. We sang hymns, we read Scripture; we supported each other and were providing the kind of spiritual environment that my very religious mother had always enjoyed. She was a deaconess, sang in the choir and was well known by all in her community as a caring person who worked in the local nursing home, the county hospital, and visited shut-ins with my father for many years. She was, briefly, a truly wonderful and giving woman. Now she was dying and we wanted to provide her with the kind of spiritual environment that she had given to so many others, including us, her children. So we drove in the bitter cold and on the icy roads to give what comfort we could to our mother who eventually became verbally non-responsive and in what appeared to be a coma. The doctor said she would not last more than twenty-four hours. This was the week before Christmas. I was about to be taught a life-changing lesson about guilt and forgiveness, by my mother.

Feelings of guilt or shame don't have to be founded upon reality to be real for the one who feels guilty. There is such a thing as false guilt, which is often based upon our memory of an action or a thought that broke rules or guidelines placed upon us by family or society. But, whether it is real or false, guilt is always powerful. For this reason, forgiveness becomes very important—and elusive. Forgiveness is not the same as being excused or let off the hook for wrongs that need to be corrected or for which amends need to be made. Guilt can be a necessary incentive that prods us to make changes that need to be made for our own sake as well as for that of others. True forgiveness isn't based upon forgetting our past, but on remembering it so that needed change can be made. Unresolved guilt, on the other hand, blocks us from remembering, and so the guilt can descend into toxic shame which is a crippling situation indeed.

Healthy forgiveness, in comparison, frees us to give up the need to blame, find fault or punish the one doing the wrong act, expecting that as a result, changes in behavior will follow. Unfortunately, we often continue to blame ourselves for past actions, and this can result in very destructive dynamics in the personality up to and including the life of the spirit. I've learned this in many ways, from many different people through the years. Forgiveness is always difficult. Forgiveness of self is often nearly impossible. We all too easily make far more excuses than are healthy. Or, more often than not, we keep our self blame inside where nobody else can witness our spiritual pain, and as a result we live our lives feeling unworthy. Outwardly we might appear almost arrogant or grandiose and not guilty at all, but inwardly we might feel very ashamed. But now, back to how my mother taught me the lesson I needed to learn.

My two sisters and my wife (who is an RN) provided the physical care and much of the emotional care for Mom during this time. The rest of us took turns sitting at the bedside or just talking with each other. During one of the times when I was sitting close to her, I visited with her as I had been trained to do as a chaplain when visiting any dying person. I said all the standard things about letting go and trusting God and being grateful for all she had given us and so forth. Suddenly, Mom's eyes opened, she looked right at me with what seemed great intensity and even displeasure or anger for a few seconds. Then her eyes closed and she resumed her coma. I was really upset because it felt like I needed to do something but I didn't know what. She seemed to be telling me something urgent but I had no idea what it was.

In any case, Mom didn't die as the doctor predicted, according to his schedule. My sister and her husband from New York needed to go home so they left. In accordance with my mother's often-stated wishes, we didn't rush her to the hospital to engage in futile efforts to save her physical life when her entire body was shutting down from the advanced cancer. Our goal of making sure Mom was kept comfortable had been achieved. But when she didn't die, we began to second guess parts of our decision. After a few days, we decided to take her to the hospital in Winchester, Kansas, where Mom had worked as a nurse's aide and the entire staff knew and loved her. There was no medical treatment that would be given beyond the comfort care already in place, but they washed and set her hair, they bathed and fussed over her but she stubbornly (?) refused to die.

It was now four days since the doctor said she had twenty-four hours to live, and yet she was still in her coma, very much with us. It was Christmas Day, and we had family in from Iowa to visit us there in Topeka. It was bitterly cold, actually around twenty degrees below zero, that day. It was so cold that the car heater could barely keep frost off of the windshield as we drove the thirty-five miles to Winchester to see my mother. As I said earlier, I was distressed by my mother's response to my visit with her and wanted very much to know what it was that she wanted or needed. As I drove, I turned to my wife and said, "Honey, I know what I need to say to Mom!" And I did know, even though it made no sense to me as I thought about it.

We arrived safely at the hospital and went in to see Mom. Carol left me alone with her after our initial arrival and so I sat by my mother, held her hand and started to talk with her about forgiveness. I said that if I had done anything to hurt her in the past I asked that she forgive me. I said that if she felt bad about anything she had done or said to me that I forgave her. I talked about forgiveness for and from others and talked about forgiveness in every dimension and direction I could. Eventually I said that if she was angry at others or even at God, she could give up that blame and forgive them. And, finally, I told her, as son and as chaplain/minister/priest, that she was forgiven by God. She made no outward response, didn't smile or squeeze my hand. There was no evidence she heard me. We returned home, to be with our family there for Christmas. In less than an hour from the time we left the hospital, we were in our home only to receive a phone call from the hospital saying that my mother had just died. So, we made the return trip to the hospital, my youngest sister drove in from Kansas City, and we called our other sister so she could make arrangements to return and help prepare for the funeral. It was now over.

As my mother requested, and planned, I did her memorial service and fulfilled her every request but one. I was unable to sing in the male quartet, so a cousin filled in for me, the son of her close friend and cousin who had been Mom's childhood chum. My father and I escorted my mother's body down to KU Medical Center where she had willed her body to be given to the medical school. The years of cancer and her battle with death had finally come to a close, **_exactly as she planned it_**. I had been unaware of what she needed but she knew full well what it was. She taught me much in life and she continued to teach me even by her death.

What did she teach me? She wanted to be forgiven. She needed to find her own forgiveness. What for? I didn't need to know the details right then. All I needed to do was to listen to her and to offer forgiveness. On the road up to the hospital it became crystal clear and even though it made no sense, I followed through and gave her what she needed. Now, it made sense why she wouldn't die on the expected schedule given by the doctor. Now it made perfect sense why she opened her eyes and looked so intently at me as she was in her coma. She felt guilty and wouldn't die until her guilt was swallowed up in forgiveness.

Remember that guilt doesn't need to be real in the sense of being based on evidence in order for it to be felt as real. To be told that we have no need to feel guilty doesn't alleviate the guilt or the shame. I learned later that there were events in my mother's life for which she felt guilty and ashamed. There was no reason for her to feel as she did—not logically, legally, or even spiritually. God didn't blame her; I would not have blamed her, but the point is that she blamed herself and she had never felt forgiven or worthy within herself. Even at those times when I as a pastor presided over a communion service and she helped prepare the elements and serve as deaconess, she didn't feel worthy. I took part in her ordination as deaconess and she was part of the laying on of hands at my ordination as a minister. But this was not all she needed. What she expected of me as her son and as her **_priest_** was for me to tell her that she was forgiven. I did that. She believed and received it and was ready to die only then. She taught me this, and I have never forgotten it. And I have never forgotten the feeling of satisfaction and fulfillment that saying those words to her gave me. They are powerful words.

So, what did I learn that terribly cold Christmas Day? People often feel guilty and need forgiveness whether or not they are consciously aware of that need. What have I done about it? Since 1989 I have never assumed that my patients are guilt free. I usually ask something like "Are you and God on good terms?" If that opens up a conversation about their spiritual life, we will eventually visit about forgiveness. Often, my patients would respond, and say, "I sure hope I'm forgiven" or something similar. When they said that, we could move on into more specifics based on their personal religious orientation and affiliation.

We all need to feel forgiven. We are often unable to ask. Or we may feel there is no point in asking because we don't deserve it. And, not only that, we can all offer forgiveness as well—to others, of course, but also to ourselves. We need to hear that we are forgiven. We need to trust the one telling us. We need to know it is God's will. Thanks, Mom, for teaching me that. You were brave enough to face your inner fears and ask for and even demand what you needed. You did not cower before your feelings of guilt; you fought your guilt like you fought your cancer. You never gave up and you never quit. And so, Mom, neither will I. Thanks. **_Now_**, you can rest in peace.

Spiritual Support

May the cobwebs of nighttime turmoil be whisked away as the light streams down

May you shake off the old memories, frustrations and confusion of the night terrors

May you feel better as the day goes on and receive new insight and strength

May your day be uncluttered and may you be unfettered as you stand tall and walk the halls

May your eyes be opened, your vision clear and may you see what is needed

May blessings be poured upon you this day like raindrops on a rose

May the hope filled scent of your presence be fragrant to all around you

Take care of you…I will be here as you have need…if I can help in any way let me know…
Candles are lit for you so thoughts will continuously be sent to the Spirit in your behalf…

As you take care of others…may you be taken care of today.

Carol A Bond

Postscript

No, this isn't the end. It is the beginning, as every day in my life is a beginning of another section in the journey down that road to real. As the old "Dragnet" TV show said back in the day, "The stories you have heard are true—only the names have been changed to protect the innocent." In my understanding of life, there are none who are totally innocent and at the same time, none of us are totally guilty. We are who we are with no excuse, no fault, and no blame. We are all responsible to BE. I find that much more difficult than to DO. In 1977, my wife told me that I could not DO chaplaincy. I had to BE a chaplain. It took me four years to even begin to understand that, and as I shared in one of the chapters in this book, it happened when I baptized an infant after a very difficult night on duty. As I reflect on what I have learned, it seems my growth comes in the midst of some significant turmoil. I do recognize that I am more than a little bit stubborn, so maybe others learn more easily than do I.

May God's peace rest upon us all.
Cliff Bond, chaplain
Topeka, Kansas

Suggested reading, all available at Amazon.com

- **Chronicles of Narnia Box Set** by C. S. Lewis (Paperback – Oct 26, 2010)
- **Crisis and Story: Introduction to the Old Testament** by W. Lee Humphreys (Jan 1, 1990)
- **Crisis Experience in Modern Life: Theory and Theology for Pastoral Care** by Charles V. Gerkin (Dec 19, 1989)
- **Cry Babel: The nightmare of aphasia and a courageous woman's struggle to rebuild her life** by April Oursler Armstrong (Hardcover – 1979)
- **Ethics** by Dietrich Bonhoeffer (Sep 1, 1995)
- **Everyday Life in Bible Times (National Geographic Society)** by James B. Pritchard (1967)
- **J.R.R. Tolkien Boxed Set (The Hobbit and The Lord of the Rings)** by J. R. R. Tolkien (Sep 12, 1986)
- **On Death and Dying (Scribner Classics)** by Elisabeth Kubler-Ross (Jul 2, 1997)
- **Pascal's Pensees** by Blaise Pascal (Feb 18, 2012)
- **Pastoral Counseling** by Wayne Edward Oates (Jan 1, 1981)
- **Salvation and health;: The interlocking processes of life,** by James N. Lapsley (1972)

- ✓ <u>The Earthsea Trilogy: A Wizard of Earthsea; The Tombs of Atuan; The Farthest Shore</u> by Ursula K. Le Guin (Hardcover – 2005)
- ✓ <u>The New Testament: An Expanded Translation</u> by Kenneth Wuest (Oct 12, 1994)
- ✓ <u>The Velveteen Rabbit (Dover Children's Classics)</u> by Margery Williams and William Nicholson (Nov 17, 2011)
- ✓ <u>The Wounded Healer: Ministry in Contemporary Society</u> by Henri J. M. Nouwen (Paperback – Nov 1994)
- ✓ <u>Turning Points in Pastoral Care: The Legacy of Anton Boisen and Seward Hiltner (Psychology and Christianity, 4)</u> by Leroy Aden and J. Harold Ellens (Apr 1990)
- ✓ <u>Vine's Complete Expository Dictionary of Old and New Testament Words: With Topical Index</u> by W. E. Vine and Merrill F. Unger (Aug 28, 1996)

CPSIA information can be obtained at www.ICGtesting.com
Printed in the USA
LVOW11s0037080314

376494LV00002B/2/P